The COMMERCIAL BANKING
Regulatory Handbook

1998–1999 Edition

PRICEWATERHOUSECOOPERS 🅿️

SHARPE PROFESSIONAL
An imprint of M.E. Sharpe, INC.

Copyright © PricewaterhouseCoopers, 1999

All rights reserved. No part of this book may be reproduced in any form without written permission from the publisher, M. E. Sharpe, Inc., 80 Business Park Drive, Armonk, New York 10504

This publication is designed to provide accurate and authoritative information in regard to the subject matter covered. It is sold with the understanding that the publisher is not engaged in rendering legal, accounting, or other professional service. If legal advice or other expert assistance is required, the services of a competent professional person should be sought.

—From the Declaration of Principles jointly adopted by a Committee of the American Bar Association and a Committee of Publishers and Associations

ISBN 0-7656-0268-7
ISSN 1090-2538

Printed in the United States of America

(IPC) 10 9 8 7 6 5 4 3 2 1

TABLE OF CONTENTS

	Introduction	3
I	Interagency Safety and Soundness Guidelines	5
II.	Affiliate Transactions	9
III.	Appointment of Officers and Directors	17
IV.	Audits and Accounting Standards	21
V.	Bank Bribery Act	27
VI.	Bank Protection Act	31
VII.	Brokered Deposits	37
VIII.	Business Recovery Planning	43
IX.	Capital Adequacy	47
X.	Daylight Overdrafts	75
XI.	Dividends	81
XII.	Environmental Assessments, Compliance, and Lender Liability	87
XIII.	Foreign Asset Controls	99
XIV.	Interbank Liabilities	103
XV.	International Banking Operations	109
XVI.	Lease Financing	125
XVII.	Lending Limits	131
XVIII.	Loans Secured by Bank Stock	143
XIX.	Loans to Insiders	147
XX.	Management Interlocks	157
XXI.	Margin Loans	163
XXII.	Political Contributions	169
XXIII.	Real Estate Appraisals	173
XXIV.	Real Estate Lending Standards	179
XXV.	Real Estate Ownership	185
XXVI.	Reserves on Deposits	191
XXVII.	Tying Provisions	197
	Index	201

The COMMERCIAL BANKING
Regulatory Handbook

Introduction

The Handbook

The Regulatory Advisory Services practice of **PricewaterhouseCoopers** has prepared *The Commercial Banking Regulatory Handbook* to provide the firm and its financial institution clients with a summary of the major federal laws and regulations enforced through safety and soundness examinations by the federal financial regulatory agencies. The *Handbook* is one in a series of six Compliance Handbooks prepared by Regulatory Advisory Services, with the others focusing on Consumer, Securities, Trust, Regulatory Reporting, and Regulatory Risk Management Requirements.

Because of the frequency with which these laws and regulations are changed or new ones adopted, we revise this *Handbook* annually. The information in this *Handbook* is current as of February 1, 1998.

Readers should be cautioned that we have not discussed all the myriad laws and regulations affecting an institution's safe and sound operation. We focus instead on those laws and regulations that typically are the focus of regulatory scrutiny, and often lead to difficulties for financial institutions. This area remains quite complex with many technical requirements and frequent and sometimes varying agency interpretations. The *Handbook* should, therefore, be used as only one resource in addition to reviewing the actual statute or regulation, or seeking additional counsel or advice.

PwC Regulatory Advisory Services

The **PricewaterhouseCoopers** Regulatory Advisory Services practice in Washington, D.C., consists of former senior federal bank regulators, attorneys, and bankers who advise their clients on a broad range of U.S. bank regulatory and supervisory issues. The group is prepared to assist any financial institution in developing an effective compliance program or in evaluating its existing compliance program. Regulatory Advisory Services also is prepared to conduct reviews of an institution's policies and procedures in a particular area as well as on-site examinations to assist the institution in evaluating its level of compliance or in preparing for a regulatory exam.

If you would like additional information about the material contained in this *Handbook*, or about the compliance services offered by **Pricewaterhouse-Coopers** Regulatory Advisory Services, please call:

Paul G. Nelson	(202) 414-4331
C. Westbrook Murphy	(202) 414-4301
Gary M. Welsh	(202) 414-4311
Paul Allan Schott	(202) 822-4272
Jeffrey P. Lavine	(202) 414-4320
David R. Sapin	(202) 414-4321
Daniel L. Weiss	(202) 414-4305
Michael VanHuysen	(202) 414-1360

I. Interagency Safety and Soundness Guidelines

Introduction and Purpose 6

Operational and Managerial Standards 6

Agencies' Existing Authority 7

Compliance Plan 7

Enforcement 8

References 8

Commercial Banking Regulatory Handbook

Introduction and Purpose

In July 1995, the federal banking agencies (the OCC, FRB, FDIC, and OTS) first adopted the Interagency Guidelines Establishing Standards for Safety and Soundness. The guidelines consisted of:

- Operational and managerial standards; and

- Compensation standards.

In August 1996, the agencies established additional standards relating to asset quality and earnings.

Congress required this action in its 1991 amendments to the Federal Deposit Insurance Act. The guidelines are designed to encourage the adoption of safe and sound banking practices appropriate to the size of the institution and the nature and scope of its activities.

Operational and Managerial Standards

Although the guidelines establish certain operational and managerial standards, they do not specify how an institution should achieve them. This flexibility allows the institution to use the method that is best suited to its size, nature, and scope of activities. An institution must meet the following operational and managerial standards.

Internal controls and information systems. An institution should have internal controls and information systems that provide clear lines of authority, effective risk assessment, and compliance with applicable laws. The design and execution of the controls should be tailored to the institution's operating environment.

Internal audit system. An institution should have an internal audit system with adequate testing and review of internal controls. A system of independent reviews may be used by an institution whose size and scope of operations does not warrant a full-scale system.

Loan documentation. An institution should establish loan documentation practices that provide for proper recording or perfection of the security interest. The documentation practices should permit different treatment according to loan type and amount.

Credit underwriting. An institution should act within the general parameters of safe and sound credit underwriting practices by evaluating the nature of the markets, the borrower, and the concentration of credit risk.

Interagency Safety and Soundness Guidelines 7

Interest rate exposure. An institution should manage interest rate risk in a manner appropriate to its size and the complexity of its assets and liabilities. The institution should establish procedures for periodic reports on risk management to the institution's management and board of directors.

Asset growth. An institution should base its asset growth on a plan that fully considers the source of the growth, the risks presented by the growth, and the effect of growth on capital. The regulatory agencies will evaluate asset growth against the institution's overall strategic plan for growth.

Compensation, fees, and benefits. An institution should maintain safeguards to assure that its compensation, fees, or benefits are not excessive and that payments will not lead to material financial loss. The agencies distinguish the requirement of safeguards from the separate standards governing the actual payment of excessive compensation, discussed below.

Asset quality. An institution should have monitoring and reporting systems to identify problem assets, prevent deterioration in those assets, and estimate inherent losses. Material concentrations of credit risk and the level of capital reserves should be considered when forming corrective action plans.

Earnings. An institution should evaluate earnings to ensure that they are sufficient to maintain adequate capital and reserves. Monitoring and reporting systems should be in place for prompt remedial action.

Agencies' Existing Authority

The provisions of this interagency rule merely provide guidance. The standards do not preclude any agency from using different criteria when determining the safety and soundness of an institution. An institution that complies with the guidelines still may be found to be in unsafe or unsound condition or to have engaged in an unsafe or unsound practice. Conversely, failure to comply with the standards does not necessarily constitute an unsafe or unsound practice, except for failure to comply with the prohibition on compensation standard.

Compliance Plan

If an agency determines that an institution fails to meet any standard under the guidelines, then it may request that the institution file a written compliance plan. This plan should include:

- A description of the steps the institution will take to correct the deficiency; and

- The time within which those steps will be taken.

Within 30 days after an agency request, the institution must submit the compliance plan to the appropriate regulator for approval.

Enforcement

Failure to properly file or adhere to the compliance plan may subject the institution to various sanctions. The agency must, by order, require the institution to correct the deficiency. This order is enforceable in court and failure to comply with it could result in civil penalties. Agencies retain the authority to pursue other, more appropriate or effective, courses of action for noncompliance. An agency may begin supervisory action against an institution even if it did not request the institution to file a compliance plan.

References

Regulations

12 CFR 30 Appendix A (OCC)
12 CFR 208 Appendix D (FRB)
12 CFR 364 Appendix A (FDIC)
12 CFR 570 Appendix A (OTS)

II. Affiliate Transactions

Introduction and Purpose 10

Section 23A 10

Covered Affiliates 10

Control 10

Exempt Affiliates 11

Covered Transactions 11

Capital Percentage Limitations 12

Collateral Requirements 12

Purchase of Low-Quality Assets 13

Exemptions to 23A Restrictions 13

Section 23B 14

Covered Affiliates 14

Covered Transactions 14

Restrictions 15

Further Restrictions for Savings Associations 15

References 16

Introduction and Purpose

Sections 23A and 23B of the Federal Reserve Act primarily limit transactions between an insured depository institution and its nonbank affiliates. These limitations generally are of three kinds:

1. Transactions (such as a loan or guarantee) that extend bank credit to an affiliate are severely limited in amount and must be fully collateralized.

2. The sale of bank assets to, or the purchase of goods or services from, an affiliate must be on terms no less favorable than the bank could obtain from an unaffiliated company.

3. Special restrictions apply to fiduciary and securities transactions.

Much less severe restrictions apply to transactions between affiliated insured depository institutions.

These limitations are intended to protect insured depository institutions and their customers from abuse in financial transactions with their affiliates.

Section 23A

Covered Affiliates

For purposes of Section 23A, an "affiliate" is defined to include:

- Any company (such as a bank holding company) that controls the bank and that company's subsidiaries;

- Any bank subsidiary of the bank;

- Any company controlled directly or indirectly by, or for the benefit of, the bank's controlling shareholders;

- Any company, including a real estate investment trust or investment company, that is sponsored or advised by the bank or by its affiliate or subsidiary; or

- Any other company determined by the Federal Reserve Board to be an affiliate.

Control

"Control" is established by:

- Direct or indirect ownership, control, or voting power of 25 percent or more of any class of voting securities;

- Controlling in any way the election of a majority of the directors or trustees; or

- A finding of control by the Federal Reserve Board after notice and opportunity for hearing.

Exempt Affiliates

Certain related companies are exempt from the definition of "affiliate" for purposes of Section 23A and therefore are not subject to the limitations. They include:

- Any nonbank subsidiary that is at least 80 percent owned by the bank;

- Any company engaged solely in the safe deposit business or holding bank premises;

- Any company engaged solely in holding obligations issued or fully guaranteed by the United States or one of its agencies; and

- Any company where control results from the exercise of rights arising out of a bona fide debt previously contracted.

Any affiliated bank that is at least 80 percent under common control, while technically an affiliate, is excluded from the Section 23A limitations, except for the sister bank restrictions noted below.

Covered Transactions

A "covered transaction" includes:

1. A loan or extension of credit to an affiliate;

2. A purchase of or an investment in securities issued by an affiliate;

3. A purchase of assets (including assets subject to repurchase) from an affiliate, unless exempted by the Federal Reserve Board;

4. The acceptance of securities issued by an affiliate as collateral for any loan; and

5. The issuance of a guarantee, acceptance, or letter of credit, including an endorsement or standby letter of credit, on behalf of an affiliate.

Capital Percentage Limitations

A bank and its subsidiaries may engage in covered transactions with an affiliate *only if*:

1. For *any one* affiliate, the aggregate amount of covered transactions with the bank and its subsidiaries will not exceed 10 percent of the bank's capital stock and surplus; and

2. For *all* affiliates, the aggregate amount of covered transactions of the bank and its subsidiaries will not exceed 20 percent of the bank's capital stock and surplus.

These limits do not apply to a loan or extension of credit fully secured by U.S. government and agency securities or by a segregated and earmarked deposit account.

Capital stock and surplus is defined as an insured depository institution's total risk-based capital (Tier I capital plus Tier II capital) together with any balance of its allowance for loan and lease losses not included in Tier II capital, based on the most recent consolidated Report of Condition and Income (i.e., Call Report).

Collateral Requirements

A bank may not lend to an affiliate or issue guarantees, acceptances, or letters of credit for the account of an affiliate unless certain collateral and margin requirements are met. Eligible collateral and margins are as follows:

1. 100 percent collateral margin if the collateral consists of U.S. government and agency securities, deposits held in the bank that are specifically segregated and earmarked, or obligations (such as notes, drafts, or acceptances) that are eligible for rediscount or purchase by a Federal Reserve Bank;

2. 110 percent margin if the collateral is composed of obligations of a state or political subdivision of a state;

3. 120 percent margin if the collateral consists of other types of debt instruments, including receivables; and

4. 130 percent margin if the collateral is composed of stocks, leases, or other real or personal property.

A low-quality asset and securities issued by an affiliate of the bank are not acceptable forms of collateral. The collateral requirements do not apply to an acceptance fully secured by attached documents or by other property not involved in the transaction, with an ascertainable market value.

Purchase of Low-Quality Assets

A bank is prohibited from purchasing a low-quality asset from any affiliate (including a sister bank) unless the bank conducted an independent credit evaluation and committed to purchase the asset before the affiliate originator acquired the asset. A "low-quality asset" is an asset:

- Rated OAEM, substandard, doubtful, or loss in the most recent regulatory examination;

- On nonaccrual;

- 30 days or more past due; or

- With its terms renegotiated because of the obligor's deteriorating financial condition.

Exemptions to 23A Restrictions

The collateral and capital percentage limitations of Section 23A do not apply to certain transactions with affiliates. However, all transactions must be conducted "on terms and conditions that are consistent with safe and sound banking practices."

The transactions exempt from the collateral and capital percentage limitations are:

1. Any transaction with a bank affiliate:

    a. That controls 80 percent or more of the voting shares of the bank (i.e., a bank parent);

    b. In which the bank controls 80 percent or more of the voting shares (i.e., a bank subsidiary of the bank); or

    c. In which 80 percent or more of the voting shares are controlled by a company that controls 80 percent or more of the voting shares of the bank (i.e., the "sister bank exemption");

2. Making deposits in an affiliated bank, domestic or foreign, in the ordinary course of correspondent business, subject to any restrictions that the Federal Reserve Board may prescribe by regulation or order;

3. Giving immediate credit for uncollected items received in the ordinary course of business;

4. Making a loan or extension of credit fully secured by obligations of, or guaranteed by, the U.S. or its agencies, or by a segregated, earmarked deposit account with the bank;

5. Purchasing securities of an affiliated bank premises or service corporation, or safe deposit company;

6. Purchasing at market value assets having a public market quotation;

7. Purchasing without recourse loans from an affiliated bank; and

8. Purchasing loans previously sold by the bank to its affiliate with recourse or under an agreement to repurchase.

Section 23B

In 1987 Congress expanded the regulation of affiliate transactions by enacting Section 23B of the Federal Reserve Act. This section imposes additional requirements on various dealings among affiliates and also prohibits certain types of affiliate transactions.

Covered Affiliates

Under Section 23B, the term "affiliate" is defined the same as in Section 23A, with one notable exception—it does not include a bank. Therefore, Section 23B does not apply to any interbank transactions.

Covered Transactions

Section 23B applies to the following transactions:

1. Any "covered transaction" that has the same definition and exemptions as in Section 23A;

2. The sale of securities or other assets to an affiliate, including assets subject to an agreement to repurchase;

3. The payment of money or furnishing of services to an affiliate under contract, lease, or otherwise;

4. Any transaction in which an affiliate acts as an agent or broker or receives a fee for its services to the bank or any other person; and

5. Any transaction or series of transactions with a third party if:

a. an affiliate has a financial interest in the third party; or

b. an affiliate is a participant in such transaction or series of transactions.

Restrictions

Section 23B expanded the restrictions of Section 23A by imposing four additional requirements:

1. **On Comparable Terms.** A bank or its subsidiary may not engage in any affiliate transactions except on comparable terms and under circumstances (including credit standards) that are substantially the same, or at least as favorable to the bank or its subsidiary, as those prevailing at the time for comparable transactions with other nonaffiliated companies.

In the absence of comparable transactions, a transaction offered to an affiliate (including credit standards) needs to be such that, in good faith, it would be offered to a nonaffiliated company.

2. **Fiduciary Purchases.** A bank or its subsidiary may not as a fiduciary purchase any securities or other assets from any affiliate *unless* permitted (1) under the instrument creating the fiduciary relationship, (2) by court order, or (3) by law of the jurisdiction governing the fiduciary relationship.

A bank will not be deemed to be a fiduciary, for this purpose, when acting as a broker.

3. **Purchases from Affiliate as Underwriter.** A bank or its subsidiary may not purchase or otherwise acquire, during the existence of any underwriting or selling syndicate, any security if a principal underwriter of that security is an affiliate of the bank *unless* the purchase or acquisition of the securities has been approved previously by a majority of the independent directors of the bank.

4. **Responsibility for Affiliate Obligations.** A bank, its subsidiary, or affiliate may not publish any advertisement or enter into any agreement stating or suggesting that the bank shall in any way be responsible for the obligations of its affiliates.

Further Restrictions for Savings Associations

In general, Sections 23A and 23B apply to savings associations, except that a savings association *may not*:

1. Extend credit to any affiliate engaged in activities that are impermissible for a bank holding company; or

2. Purchase or invest in any securities of an affiliate other than shares of a subsidiary.

References

Laws:

    12 U.S.C. 371c and 371c-1
    12 U.S.C. 1468

Regulations:

    12 CFR 563.42 (OTS)
    12 CFR 250 (FRB)

III. Appointment of Officers and Directors

Introduction and Purpose 18

Affected Institutions 18

Notice Requirement 18

Agency Action 19

Waiver of Notice Requirement 19

References 19

Introduction and Purpose

Section 914 of FIRREA grants the federal banking agencies a statutory veto power over new directors and senior executive officers of certain depository institutions and their holding companies. An affected institution must notify its regulatory agency 30 days before appointing such officers or directors.

This section covers the limitations imposed by FIRREA on the appointment of officers and directors. For a discussion on management interlocks and the recent joint agency rule, see the Management Interlocks section in this *Handbook*.

Affected Institutions

The notice requirement applies to a depository institution or its holding company that:

a. fails to comply with its minimum capital requirements;

b. is otherwise in a troubled condition; or

c. the FDIC determines must provide prior notice.

A financial institution is considered in a "troubled" condition if it:

1. Has been assigned a composite rating of 4 or 5 under the Uniform Financial Institutions Rating System;

2. Is subject to a cease-and-desist order or written agreement requiring action to improve its financial condition; or

3. Is expressly so informed by its regulatory agency.

Notice Requirement

An affected financial institution must file notice with the appropriate regulatory agency 30 days prior to adding or replacing a member of the board of directors, and prior to employing, or changing the responsibilities of, an individual in a senior executive officer or director position. Notice must be given on the agency's form, which requires extensive financial and biographical information, fingerprints, and other data.

A "senior executive officer" is any individual who exercises significant influence over, or participates in, major policy-making decisions of the financial institution without regard to title, salary, or compensation.

Appointment of Officers and Directors

Agency Action

The regulatory agency will issue a notice of disapproval if it determines that the competence, character, or integrity of the individual indicates that it would not be in the best interest of the public or the depositors of the institution for the individual to be employed by, or associated with, the institution. If no notice of disapproval is received within 90 days the individual may begin service.

Waiver of Notice Requirement

The appropriate banking agency may waive the notice requirements if the delay associated with prior notice would threaten the safety and soundness of the financial institution involved. In addition, the agency may waive the notice requirement if the delay would harm the public good or if extraordinary circumstances exist that justify such a waiver.

A waiver will not affect the authority of the agency to issue a notice of disapproval within 30 days of the waiver.

References

Laws:

    12 U.S.C. 1831i

Regulations:

    12 CFR 5.51 (OCC)
    12 CFR 225.71-.73 (FRB)
    12 CFR 303.14 (FDIC)
    12 CFR 574.9 (OTS)

IV. Audits and Accounting Standards

Introduction and Purpose 22

Audits and Attestation 22

General 22

Annual Report 22

Audited Financials 23

Management Report 23

Independent Public Accountants 24

Engaging and Terminating an IPA 24

IPA Qualifications 24

Audit Committee 24

Holding Company Exception 25

Accounting Standards 26

General 26

References 26

22   Commercial Banking Regulatory Handbook

Introduction and Purpose

The FDIC requires each bank and savings association over a certain size to file an annual report containing audited financial statements and a report on internal controls and compliance. FDIC and its sister regulatory agencies also possess the power to mandate bank and savings association accounting rules that are stricter than generally accepted accounting principles. These auditing and accounting provisions are intended to lead to early recognition of difficulties that, if not addressed, could cause losses to the deposit insurance funds.

Audits and Attestation

General

The FDIC regulations implementing Section 36 of the Federal Deposit Insurance Act apply to each FDIC-insured depository institution with assets in excess of $500 million at the beginning of its fiscal year ("covered institution").

The regulation and its accompanying guidelines require:

- Annual management reports;

- Independent audit committees; and

- Audits and attestations by independent accountants meeting specified qualifications.

A savings association must follow the above guidelines if it has:

- A composite CAMELS rating of 3, 4, or 5; or

- Assets of $500 million or more.

As of December 1994, a small savings association with assets of less than $500 million and a composite CAMELS rating of 1 or 2 is exempt from the mandatory audit requirements. OTS has reserved the right to require an independent audit whenever safety and soundness concerns arise.

Annual Report

Each covered institution must file an annual report with the FDIC and its other appropriate state or federal bank regulators within 90 days after the end of its fiscal year.

Audits and Accounting Standards

The annual report must include:

1. Audited financial statements;
2. A management report; and
3. An independent public accountant's attestation report on internal control structure and procedures for financial reporting.

The institution separately must file an independent accountant's attestation report on the institution's compliance with designated laws.

Audited Financials

The financial statements of each covered institution must be prepared annually in accordance with generally accepted accounting principles (GAAP) and be audited by an independent public accountant. Institutions that are subsidiaries of holding companies may satisfy the annual audit requirement by filing the audited financial statements of the holding company.

Management Report

Each covered institution annually must prepare a management report, signed by its chief executive and chief financial officers, that contains:

1. A statement of management's responsibilities for:

    a. preparing the annual financial statements;

    b. establishing and maintaining an adequate internal control structure and procedures for financial reporting; and

    c. complying with particular laws designated by the FDIC as affecting the safety and soundness of insured depositories; and

2. Assessments by management of:

    a. the effectiveness of the institution's internal control structure and procedures as of the end of the fiscal year; and

    b. the institution's compliance, during such fiscal year, with the designated safety and soundness laws.

The designated safety and soundness laws currently are limited to:

- Federal laws and regulations concerning loans to insiders; and

- Federal and state laws and regulations concerning restrictions on the payment of dividends.

Independent Public Accountants

Each covered institution is required to engage an independent public accountant (IPA) to audit and report on its annual financial statements in accordance with generally accepted auditing standards.

The institution's IPA also must examine, attest to, and report separately on management's assertions about internal controls. The attestation is to be made in accordance with generally accepted standards for attestation engagements. An earlier requirement for an IPA to attest to the institution's compliance report was dropped in 1996.

Engaging and Terminating an IPA

A covered institution must notify both the FDIC and its primary state or federal regulator within 15 days of engaging or changing an IPA to perform services required by FDIC regulation. A notice about changing accountants must state the reasons for the change, and a copy must be sent to the former or resigning IPA. The former IPA has 15 days to inform the agency if it agrees with the reasons given for termination.

IPA Qualifications

An IPA performing the required services must be subject to a professional peer review and meet other qualifications. The IPA must:

- Send the regulators names of the covered institutions for which it provides services;

- Provide the regulators a copy of its peer review; and

- Agree to make its work papers available to the regulators.

Audit Committee

Each covered institution's board of directors must have an audit committee entirely composed of directors who are independent of management, unless a federal supervisory agency permits otherwise. The audit committee is required to review with management and the IPA the basis for the reports required by the FDIC's regulation.

Audits and Accounting Standards 25

With the permission of its federal supervisory agency, an audit committee may include one or more directors (but not less than a majority) who are not independent. The agency must find that the institution encountered hardships in retaining and recruiting a sufficient number of outside directors to serve on the committee. In making its finding, the agency will consider:

- The size of the institution; and

- Whether the institution made a good faith effort to elect or name additional competent outside directors to the board who qualify to serve on the audit committee.

The audit committee of any insured institution that has total assets in excess of $3 billion, measured as of the beginning of each fiscal year, must:

- Include at least two members with banking or related financial management expertise;

- Have access to its own outside counsel; and

- Not include any large customer of the institution.

A **large customer** includes any individual or entity that the board of directors believes to have such significant credit or other relationships with the institution, the termination of which likely would materially and adversely affect the institution's financial condition or results of operation.

If an institution relies on the audit committee of a holding company to comply with this rule, the holding company audit committee cannot include any members who are large customers of the institution.

Holding Company Exception

The requirements of the FDIC's regulation, in some instances, may be satisfied by a bank's or savings association's parent holding company. The requirement for audited financial statements always may be satisfied by providing audited financial statements of the consolidated holding company. The other requirements may be satisfied by the holding company if:

1. The services and functions comparable to those required of the depository institution are provided at the holding company level; and

2. Either the depository institution has total assets as of the beginning of the fiscal year of:

a. less than $5 billion; or

b. more than $5 billion *and* a composite CAMELS rating of 1 or 2.

The institution is allowed to use the audit committee of its holding company and can file the committee's annual report instead of its own.

The appropriate federal banking agency may revoke the holding company exception for any institution with total assets over $9 billion if the agency determines that the institution's exemption would create a significant risk to the affected deposit insurance fund. The nonexempt institution must have its own audit committee and report separately from the holding company.

Accounting Standards

General

Companion legislation "Section 121 of the Federal Deposit Insurance Corporation Improvement Act of 1991 (FDICIA)" requires uniform and consistent GAAP accounting standards at all insured depository institutions. However, the federal banking agencies may determine that the application of any GAAP principle to any insured institution with respect to any regulatory report or statement is inconsistent with congressional objectives, and may prescribe an accounting principle that is "no less stringent" than GAAP.

The federal banking agencies are directed to:

- Evaluate their current reporting requirements and modify them to conform to GAAP;

- Establish uniform standards for determining capital ratios and other reporting purposes; and

- Develop, to the extent feasible, a method for supplemental disclosure of the fair market value of assets and liabilities.

References

Laws:

  12 U.S.C. 1831m and 1831n

Regulations:

  12 CFR Part 363 (FDIC)
  12 CFR Part 562 (OTS)

V. Bank Bribery Act

Introduction and Purpose 28

Prohibitions 28

Permitted Activities 28

Penalties 28

Agency Guidelines 28

References 29

Introduction and Purpose

The Bank Bribery Act forbids either offering or soliciting anything of value with a corrupt intent to influence any transaction or business of a financial institution. The Act applies to all banks, saving associations, their holding companies, and their agents or attorneys.

Prohibitions

The Bank Bribery Act affects the corrupt conduct of bankers and their customers.

Prohibited conduct by a banker. An officer, director, employee, agent, or attorney of a financial institution may not solicit, accept, or demand, for the benefit of any person, anything of value from any person intending to be influenced or rewarded in connection with any business or transaction of that institution.

Prohibited conduct by a customer. An individual may not give, offer, or promise anything of value to any person with intent to influence or reward an officer, director, employee, agent, or attorney of a financial institution in connection with any business or transaction of that institution.

Permitted Activities

The statute permits payment of bona fide salary, wages, fees, and expenses. The statute also permits a bank agent or officer to demand, accept, and solicit payments to the bank itself.

Penalties

If the value of the bribe or gratuity offered or received exceeds $100, the offense is a felony punishable by a fine of up to $1 million or three times the value of the bribe or gratuity, whichever is greater, or by up to 20 years imprisonment, or both.

If the value does not exceed $100, the offense is a misdemeanor punishable by up to one year imprisonment or a maximum fine of $1,000, or both.

Agency Guidelines

An interagency working group in 1987 developed guidelines that encourage financial institutions to adopt internal codes of conduct to explain the general prohibitions of the bank bribery law and to establish standards for bank employees.

The guidelines also provide examples where a bank official, without risk of corruption or breach of trust, may accept something of value from someone doing or seeking to do business with the bank. The most common examples are the business luncheon or the holiday season gift from a customer.

In addition to maintaining a written copy of its code of conduct, the guidelines recommend that the financial institution obtain a signed statement from its officials acknowledging receipt of the code of conduct and their agreement to comply. The institution also should maintain contemporaneous written reports of any disclosures made by its officials in connection with the code of conduct or written policy.

References

Laws:

    18 U.S.C. 215

Guidelines:

    OCC: Comptroller's Handbook "Insider Activities"
    FRB: SR 87-36 (FIS) (Oct. 30, 1987)
    FDIC: FDIC Notice (Nov. 17, 1987)
    OTS: FHLBB Policy Statement, Res. No. 88-209 (Mar. 15, 1988)

VI. Bank Protection Act

Introduction and Purpose 32

Security Officer 32

Security Program 32

Security Devices 32

Annual Report to Board 33

Recordkeeping Requirements 33

Suspicious Activity Reporting 33

Filing of Forms 34

Mailing Instructions 36

References 36

32 Commercial Banking Regulatory Handbook

Introduction and Purpose

The Bank Protection Act of 1968 (BPA) represents an effort to control the incidence of crimes against financial institutions. The Act requires the federal financial regulatory agencies to create rules and regulations establishing minimum security standards, such as the installation, maintenance, and operation of security devices. The agencies have adopted substantially similar regulations.

Security Officer

A financial institution's board of directors must designate a security officer who is responsible for developing and administering a written security program to protect the association's principal office and all branch offices from robberies, burglaries, and nonemployee larcenies.

The security officer also is responsible for employee training regarding security devices and procedures.

Security Program

Every institution's security program must include procedures for:

- Daily opening and closing of offices;

- Safekeeping of currency and similar valuables;

- Assisting in identifying persons committing crimes against the institution;

- Initial and periodic training of employees in their responsibilities under the security program; and

- Selecting, testing, operating, and maintaining appropriate security devices, including those listed below.

Security Devices

Regulations require all banks and savings associations to employ the following four minimum security devices:

- A secure space for cash;

- A lighting system for illuminating the vault, if the vault is visible from outside the office;

- An alarm system; and

- Tamper-resistant locks on exterior doors and windows.

The security officer is responsible for selecting the additional security devices that will best meet the needs of the institution.

Annual Report to Board

The security officer must report at least annually on the effectiveness of the bank's security program. This report must be delivered to the bank's board of directors and reflected in the minutes.

The report must include such information as the:

- Status of employee training;

- Number of offenses against the bank; and

- Success of prosecution for such offenses.

Recordkeeping Requirements

Institutions must keep complete and accurate security records. These records include:

- A copy of the current security program, approved by the board of directors, including evidence of board appointment of the institution's security officer;

- Records of periodic testing and servicing of security devices;

- Maintenance contracts;

- Statement of the reasons for deciding not to install security devices that are at least equivalent to standards established by the regulations; and

- Records regarding the incidence of a robbery, burglary, larceny, theft, fraud, or other crime, suspected crime, or unexplained loss.

Suspicious Activity Reporting

Financial institutions must promptly report any crime, suspected crime, or unexplained loss to appropriate law enforcement and regulatory agencies. In

February 1996, the FDIC, FRB, OCC, and OTS adopted a Suspicious Activity Report (SAR) (for more details on the form, see *The Regulatory Reporting Handbook*). The SAR replaces the various Criminal Referral Forms from each of the federal regulatory agencies and provides a consistent means by which financial institutions can inform law enforcement of any known or suspected criminal activity perpetrated against or through the institution.

An institution must file a SAR no later than 30 calendar days after discovering a known or suspected criminal violation or suspicious financial transaction. The institution may delay filing for an additional 30 days if it did not identify a suspect on the date it discovered the violation or suspicious transaction. The institution may not delay reporting more than 60 calendar days after discovery.

Filing of Forms

An institution must file the SAR following the discovery of:

- **Suspected insider abuse involving any amount.** An institution must report any potential federal criminal violation on the SAR, regardless of the amount involved, where the institution believes that it was either a potential victim of a violation or was used to facilitate a criminal transaction and the bank has a "substantial basis" for identifying one of its directors, officers, employees, agents, or other institution-affiliated party as having participated in a criminal act.

- **Transactions aggregating $5,000 or more where suspect can be identified.** An institution must file a SAR for transactions aggregating to $5,000 or more in funds or other assets where the institution suspects that it was a potential victim of a federal criminal violation or was used to facilitate a criminal transaction *and* the institution has a "substantial basis" for identifying a suspect or group of suspects.

- **Transactions aggregating $25,000 or more regardless of potential suspects.** An institution must file a SAR for transactions aggregating to $25,000 or more in funds or other assets where the institution suspects that it was a potential victim of a federal criminal violation or was used to facilitate a criminal transaction, even though the institution does not have a substantial basis for identifying a possible suspect or group of suspects.

- **Transactions aggregating $5,000 or more that involve potential money laundering or violations of the Bank Secrecy Act.** An institution must file a SAR for any transaction conducted or attempted by, at, or through the institution and involving or aggregating to $5,000 or more in funds or other assets, if the institution suspects or has reason to suspect that the transaction:

- involves funds derived from illegal activity or is intended to hide funds or other assets derived from illegal activities as part of a plan to evade any federal law, regulation, or transaction reporting requirements;

- is designed to evade any Bank Secrecy Act regulations; or

- has no business or apparent lawful purpose or is not the sort in which the customer would normally be expected to engage, and the institution knows of no reasonable explanation for the transaction.

Institutions are not required to file a SAR for robberies and burglaries that are reported to local authorities, or for lost, missing, counterfeit, or stolen securities that are otherwise appropriately reported.

Where violations require immediate attention (e.g., when a reportable violation is ongoing), the bank must immediately notify, by telephone, an appropriate law enforcement authority and its federal regulatory agency in addition to filing a timely SAR.

An institution may be required to file a SAR if certain criminal statutes are violated. For a list of these statutes, see the Suspicious Activity Report section in *The Regulatory Reporting Handbook.*

Record Retention

Institutions must retain for five years from the date of filing, a copy of any SAR filed and the original or business record equivalent of supporting documentation. Although no supporting documentation is filed with the SAR, institutions must make all supporting documentation available to appropriate law enforcement agencies upon request.

Notification of Board of Directors

Management must promptly notify its board of directors, or a committee designated by the board, of any SAR that was filed.

Safe Harbor

The safe harbor of the Right to Financial Privacy Act exempts from liability under any federal or state law or regulation, disclosures made in good faith of any possible violation of law or regulation. The safe harbor protects both mandatory and voluntary disclosures made within the parameters specified in the Act.

Confidentiality of SARs

Under the SAR rules, an institution which is subpoenaed or otherwise requested to disclose information is prohibited from producing a SAR or providing any information that would disclose that a SAR had been prepared or filed. The institution requested to provide information must notify its federal regulator of the request.

Mailing Instructions

An institution must file the SAR with the Financial Crimes Enforcement Network of the Department of the Treasury:

FinCEN
P. O. Box 32621
Detroit, MI 48232

FinCEN will distribute relevant information to the appropriate authorities, including the U.S. Secret Service, Financial Crimes Division, for credit card and computer fraud. An institution should not file a copy of the SAR with the U.S. Secret Service or the banking regulators.

References

Laws:

12 U.S.C. 1881 et seq.

Regulations:

12 CFR Part 21 (OCC)
12 CFR Parts 208 (FRB)
12 CFR Parts 326, 353 (FDIC)
12 CFR Part 568 (OTS)

VII. Brokered Deposits

Introduction and Purpose 38

Prohibitions 38

Definitions 38

Exceptions 40

Waivers 40

Broker Notification 41

References 41

Introduction and Purpose

FIRREA restricted an insured depository institution's authority to accept brokered deposits if it does not meet minimum capital requirements. FDICIA further tightened the restrictions on brokered deposits. A brokered deposit includes not only deposits solicited or received through a broker, but also deposits that pay more than 75 basis points above the prevailing market rate in the institution's market.

The intent of the restriction is to prevent an undercapitalized institution from using brokered deposits to support unsound or rapid expansion of its loan and investment portfolio and from destabilizing interest rates in its market.

Prohibitions

Under FDICIA, an institution's authority to solicit and accept brokered deposits depends on the institution's level of capital compliance with the new categories created by the Act.

- **Well-capitalized** institutions may accept brokered deposits without prior FDIC approval.

- **Adequately capitalized** institutions are prohibited from accepting brokered deposits unless they first obtain a waiver from the FDIC. However, a waiver does not permit adequately capitalized banks to pay rates of interest on deposits that are significantly higher than regional or national market rates.

- **Undercapitalized** institutions are prohibited from accepting any brokered deposits; no waiver is permitted. They also are prohibited from soliciting deposits by offering rates significantly higher than those prevailing in their normal market area.

Definitions

Well-capitalized, adequately capitalized, and **undercapitalized**. The same definitions apply for brokered deposits as apply for the Prompt Corrective Action regulations.

Classifications are made according to the capital ratios shown on page 39.

Brokered deposits. Any account obtained or placed by or through a deposit broker, which can include a bank's own money desk.

PCA Capital Categories	Total Risk-Based Ratio	Tier I Risk-Based Ratio	Leverage Ratio
Well-Capitalized	≥ 10%	≥ 6%	≥ 5%
Adequately Capitalized	≥ 8%	≥ 4%	≥ 4%*
Undercapitalized	< 8%	< 4%	< 4%*

* 3.0 for 1-rated banks

Deposit broker:

- Any person engaged in the business of placing deposits, facilitating the placement of deposits, or placing deposits with insured depository institutions for the purpose of selling interests in those deposits;

- An agent or trustee who establishes a deposit account to fund a prearranged loan; or

- Any insured depository institution and any employee of any insured depository institution that solicits deposits by offering significantly higher rates of interest than the prevailing rates of interest by similarly chartered depository institutions in its normal market area.

Deposit broker does *not* include:

- A depository institution or an employee of a depository institution with respect to solicitations of deposits at market rates;

- A trust department of a depository institution or trustee of an irrevocable trust if the trust has not been established for the primary purpose of placing funds with that depository institution;

- The trustee, plan administrator, or investment adviser of a pension or other employee benefit plan with respect to funds of the plan;

- A trustee of a testamentary account;

- A trustee or custodian of a pension or a profit-sharing plan; or

- An agent or nominee whose primary purpose is not the placement of funds with depository institutions.

Significantly higher. A rate of interest that is more than 75 basis points higher than the prevailing rate offered on comparable deposits by other depository institutions. Odd maturity deposits are compared with deposits of the next longer or shorter maturities offered in the market.

Exceptions

An institution in FDIC conservatorship will not be subject to the brokered deposit prohibitions and therefore may accept brokered deposits for 90 days after the date on which the institution was placed in conservatorship. However, such institutions are still prohibited from offering rates of interest that are significantly higher than market rates.

Waivers

The FDIC may grant waivers only to institutions that are "adequately capitalized." No waivers to the brokered deposit restrictions may be made for "undercapitalized" institutions. The waiver application must include the following information:

- The time period for which the waiver is needed;

- A statement of the policy governing the use of brokered deposits in the institution's overall funding and liquidity management program;

- The volume, rates, and maturities associated with the brokered deposits held currently and anticipated during the waiver period sought, including any internal limits placed on terms, solicitation, and use of brokered deposits;

- A description of the total cost of brokered deposits compared to other funding alternatives and how such deposits are used in the institution's lending and investment activities, including a detailed discussion of any plans for asset growth;

- A description of the procedures and practices used to solicit brokered deposits, including an identification of the principal sources of such deposits;

- A description of the management systems used to oversee the solicitation acceptance and the use of brokered deposits;

- A recent consolidated financial statement with balance sheet and income statements; and

- Reasons the institution believes its acceptance, renewal, or rollover of brokered deposits will pose no undue risk.

Broker Notification

A deposit broker must register with the FDIC before it may solicit or place deposits with an insured institution. Similarly, if a deposit broker will no longer be acting as a deposit broker, it must notify the FDIC. The FDIC has issued regulations which place recordkeeping and reporting requirements on deposit brokers. A deposit broker must maintain records showing the volume of deposits placed with an insured institution over the preceding 12 months. Those records also must show the maturities, rates, and cost associated with these deposits.

References

Laws:

12 U.S.C. 1831f

Regulations:

12 CFR 337.6 (FDIC)

VIII. Business Recovery Planning

Introduction and Purpose 44

Policy Requirements 44

Board of Directors and Management Responsibilities 44

Service Bureaus 45

Planning Process 45

References 46

Introduction and Purpose

A business recovery plan addresses methods for a financial institution to withstand, and recover from, a physical or other disaster that disrupts its operations. The plan should establish strategies to:

- Minimize disruptions of service to the institution and its customers;

- Minimize financial loss; and

- Ensure a timely resumption of operations in the event of a disaster.

The Federal Financial Institutions Examination Council (FFIEC) has issued a Policy Statement that addresses the need for corporate-wide contingency planning by all financial institutions and their servicers. This statement has been adopted by all of the federal financial regulatory agencies.

Policy Requirements

The FFIEC Policy Statement requires financial institutions to develop strategies to minimize loss and to recover from significant disruptions in business operations. These strategies should address:

- Centralized and decentralized operations;

- User department activities;

- Communications systems (data and voice);

- Functions linked to service bureaus; and

- Recovery plans by the service bureaus.

Board of Directors and Management Responsibilities

A financial institution's board of directors and senior management should be responsible for:

- Establishing policies, procedures, and responsibilities for comprehensive contingency planning; and

- Reviewing and approving contingency plans annually and documenting the reviews in board minutes.

Business Recovery Planning

Service Bureaus

If a financial institution receives information processing from service bureaus, management should:

- Evaluate the adequacy of contingency plans for its service bureau; and

- Ensure that the financial institution's contingency plan is compatible with its service bureau's plan.

Planning Process

The FFIEC Policy Statement recommends that the disaster contingency planning process include:

- Obtaining a commitment from senior management to develop the plan;

- Establishing a management group to oversee development and implementation of the plan;

- Performing a risk assessment that considers possible natural (fires, flood, earthquakes, etc.), technical (hardware/software failure, power disruption, etc.), and human (riots, strikes, disgruntled employees, etc.) threats;

- Assessing impacts from loss of information and services on financial condition, competitive position, customer confidence, and legal/regulatory requirements;

- Evaluating critical needs such as functional operations, key personnel, information, processing systems, documentation, vital records, and policies/procedures;

- Assessing the response capability of key disaster recovery service vendors (e.g., vendors providing alternate processing sites; storage and transportation of backup media among the storage vendor, alternate processing site and the institution);

- Establishing priorities for recovery based on critical needs;

- Creating strategies to recover facilities, hardware, software, communications, data files, customer services, user operations, MIS, end-user systems, and other processing operations;

- Obtaining written backup agreements or contracts for facilities, hardware, software, vendor services, suppliers, disaster recovery services, and reciprocal agreements; and

- Establishing criteria for testing and maintenance of contingency plans.

Additional guidelines are available in Sections 5 and 7 of *The FFIEC Electronic Data Processing (EDP) Examination Handbook.*

References

FFIEC Interagency Policy Statement on Corporate Business Resumption and Contingency Planning (March 26, 1997); OCC Banking Circular 177 (Rev.); and SR 97-15 (FRB)

IX. Capital Adequacy

Introduction and Purpose 49

Risk-Based Capital Adequacy Standards 50

Introduction 50

Expect Risk Management Changes in 1998 50

Definition of Capital 51

Deductions 53

Goodwill 54

Qualifying Intangible Assets 54

Servicing Rights 55

Deferred Tax Assets 55

Risk-Weighted Assets 56

Introduction 56

Risk Weights for Balance Sheet Assets 56

Mutual Funds 60

Assets Sold with Recourse 60

Credit Conversion of and Risk Weights for Off-Balance
    Sheet Assets 61

48 Commercial Banking Regulatory Handbook

Interest Rate, Foreign Exchange Rate, and
  Commodity Contracts 63

Exclusions 63

Netting 64

Calculation of Credit Equivalent Amounts 64

Risk Weights for Interest Rate, Foreign Exchange, and
  Commodity Contracts 66

Interest Rate Risk 66

Market Risk Rule 67

Minimum Leverage Ratio Requirement 69

Introduction and Purpose 69

Agency Requirements 69

Prompt Corrective Action Categories 70

Introduction 70

The Five Capital Categories 70

Mandated Corrective Actions 71

Determining a Bank or Thrift Capital Category 72

"Well-Capitalized" Bank Holding Companies 73

References 74

Capital Adequacy

Introduction and Purpose

U.S. bank supervisors have established capital adequacy guidelines based on minimum capital standards for multinational banks adopted by the Basle Committee of Bank Supervisors (the "Basle Committee"). These standards:

- Define capital;

- Establish ratios of capital to assets; and

- Weight assets and credit equivalent amounts of off-balance sheet items from 0 percent to 100 percent to reflect their relative credit risk.

In the U.S., these international risk-weighted capital adequacy guidelines apply not only to banks, but also to savings associations and bank holding companies. U.S. regulators additionally require the capital of these institutions to meet minimum leverage ratios, based on unweighted total on-balance sheet assets.

In using these standards for supervisory purposes, U.S. regulators assign each FDIC insured depository institution to one of five capital categories:

- Well-Capitalized

- Adequately Capitalized

- Undercapitalized

- Significantly Undercapitalized

- Critically Undercapitalized

Institutions falling in the last three of these categories are subject to a variety of "prompt corrective actions," including limitations on dividend payments to stockholders, prohibition on acquisitions and branching, restrictions on asset growth, and removal of directors and executive officers. These sanctions do not apply directly to bank holding companies.

The Federal Reserve Board also applies less stringent supervision to bank holding companies that are "well capitalized" under both risk-weighted and leverage standards.

Risk-Based Capital Adequacy Standards

Introduction

The Basle Committee had two prime goals in pursuing a universal approach to capital adequacy:

- To strengthen the soundness and stability of the international banking system; and

- To remove a possible regulatory source of competitive inequality among international banks by establishing a universally accepted definition of capital.

In the United States, the risk-based capital standards apply to:

- Banks;

- Savings associations; and

- Bank holding companies with consolidated assets of $150 million or more.

Each of these entities must meet two risk-based minimum ratios:

- Tier I (or "core") capital: 4 percent of total risk-weighted assets; and

- Total capital: 8 percent of total risk-weighted assets.

Regulators may require any particular institution to maintain higher ratios, doing so either through informal negotiations or understandings, or through formal directives or orders. Reasons for demanding higher capital ratios could include concerns about liquidity, management quality, asset quality, credit concentrations, earnings capacity, or interest rate risk.

Expect Risk Management Changes in 1998

> Look for other changes in the next year, especially changes in the recourse and servicing rights rules.

The banking and thrift regulatory agencies recently proposed several modifications to the risk-based capital rules addressing:

- Recourse and third-party credit enhancements associated with asset securitizations;

- Inclusion in Tier II capital of a portion of pretax net unrealized holding gains on certain available-for-sale equity securities; and

Capital Adequacy

- Treatment of servicing rights.

These proposals were prompted partly by the agencies' desire to conform regulatory financial reporting with generally accepted accounting principles, and by the adoption of FAS 125 "Accounting for Transfers and Servicing of Financial Assets and Extinguishments of Liabilities."

If adopted, the "recourse" rule revision introduces credit ratings to help differentiate risk-weighting and may make third-party credit enhancement more expensive, especially if the third party is subject to the risk-based capital rules. The "servicing" proposal would increase the qualifying amounts of mortgage servicing that count in regulatory capital, but does not permit inclusion of other financial asset servicing rights. Institutions affected by these proposals will wish to monitor them closely.

Tier I Leverage Ratio for Bank Holding Companies

Effective June 30, 1998, the Federal Reserve has changed its Tier I capital-to-assets ("leverage ratio") standard for bank holding companies. The final rule establishes a minimum leverage ratio of 3.0 percent for bank holding companies which have a BOPEC composite rating of 1 or which have implemented the Board's capital market risk measure of its "Capital Adequacy Guidelines." For bank holding companies that do not fit those critera, the Federal Reserve now requires a leverage ratio of at least 4.0 percent.

Definition of Capital

Total risk-based capital consists of Tier I and Tier II capital, less required deductions.

Tier I Capital (core capital)

Core capital (the numerator of the Tier I ratio) consists of the following:

- Common stock;
- Surplus;
- Undivided profits;
- Minority interests in consolidated subsidiaries;
- Qualifying perpetual preferred stock; and
- Net unrealized holding losses on available-for-sale equity securities with readily determinable fair values.

For banks, noncumulative perpetual preferred stock is counted as Tier I capital, but may not be the dominant core capital element. Other forms of preferred stock or excess amounts of qualifying noncumulative perpetual preferred stock may be counted as Tier II capital.

Bank holding companies may include noncumulative perpetual preferred stock in Tier I capital without limit, and also may count cumulative perpetual preferred stock up to 25 percent of Tier I capital.

Savings associations may add to their Tier I capital certain pledged deposits and nonwithdrawable accounts.

Tier II Capital (supplementary capital)

Total capital (the numerator for the total capital ratio) consists of core capital (defined above), plus supplementary (Tier II) capital, as follows:

- General loan loss reserves;

- Cumulative perpetual preferred stock;

- Long-term preferred stock;

- Qualifying intermediate-term preferred stock and term subordinated debt; and

- Perpetual debt and other hybrid debt/equity instruments.

These supplementary capital elements will count as part of a bank's total capital base — but only to a maximum of 100 percent of Tier I capital. Stated differently, for regulatory purposes, Tier II capital may not be larger than Tier I capital.

Cumulative perpetual preferred stock includable in Tier II capital may not be redeemable at the option of the holder.

The FRB, FDIC, and OCC limit the recognition as Tier II capital of intermediate-term preferred stock and term subordinated debt to 50 percent of Tier I capital, net of goodwill. All of these agencies require limited-life capital investments to be discounted on a straight-line basis during the five years preceding maturity (i.e., 20 percent each year on a cumulative basis). The OTS allows savings associations an alternative, which permits full inclusion of all limited-life capital instruments, provided that in aggregate they do not exceed 20 percent of a thrift's capital in any one year.

Capital Adequacy

As of September 1992, the FRB repealed its requirement that state member banks apply for permission to issue subordinated debt, and published guidance for banks and bank holding companies on the characteristics of qualifying subordinated debt to be treated as supplementary capital. Subordinated debt issued prior to September 14, 1992, that does not fully meet these characteristics may continue to qualify for regulatory capital at the discretion of the FRB.

General loan loss reserves may be included in Tier II capital, but are limited to 1.25 percent of risk-weighted assets. The agencies have determined that loan loss reserves attributable to the impairment analysis performed in accordance with FAS 114 "Accounting by Creditors for Impairment of a Loan" may be reported as general reserves, unless otherwise directed.

Deductions

Core and total risk-based capital are reduced by a number of deductions. These deductions also are subtracted from total risk-weighted assets.

The following items should be subtracted from both the numerator and the denominator when calculating the risk-based capital ratios:

- Goodwill;

- Other disallowed intangibles (e.g., core deposit intangibles);

- Portions of qualifying intangible assets (e.g., mortgage servicing rights and purchased credit card receivables) exceeding regulatory limits;

- Portions of qualifying subordinated debt and limited-life preferred stock exceeding 50 percent of a bank's Tier I capital;

- Investments in unconsolidated banking and finance subsidiaries;

- Reciprocal holdings of the capital instruments of other banking organizations;

- Certain tax assets;

- Unrealized losses on available-for-sale debt securities and on equity securities with readily determinable fair values; and

- Unrealized gains on available-for-sale debt and equity securities to the extent those gains are reflected in equity capital in accordance with FAS 115.

The agencies are proposing to reduce this deduction to 55 percent of the unrealized gain, thus permitting institutions to include in Tier II capital up to 45 percent of pre-tax net unrealized holding gains on legally held available-for-sale equity securities having a readily determinable fair market value. This modification is consistent with the Basle Committee standard framework.

Goodwill

The banking agencies' guidelines require the deduction of all goodwill, with a limited exception for state-chartered commercial banks for goodwill acquired in supervisory mergers of troubled or failed depository institutions prior to April 1989. This supervisory goodwill represents the difference between the value of the assets and liabilities of institutions acquired in supervisory transactions, and must be approved by the bank's primary regulator to be included in Tier I capital.

Qualifying Intangible Assets

As a general rule, bank regulators require the deduction of all intangible assets from Tier I capital. However, the regulators permit two types of intangible assets to be recognized as capital: mortgage servicing rights (MSR) and purchased credit card relationships (PCCR). The agencies believe that these assets:

- Are separable and salable apart from the bank or from the bulk of the bank's assets;

- Can sustain their market value irrespective of the future prospects of the financial institution, based on the certainty of readily identifiable cash flows; and

- Have a market sufficiently deep to provide liquidity for the intangible asset.

The agencies *limit* the amount of MSR and PCCR that may be recognized as Tier I capital to an aggregate of 50 percent of Tier I capital after goodwill and all other nonqualifying intangibles are deducted. There is a 25 percent sub-limit for PCCRs. Any amounts of these qualifying intangibles exceeding these limits are deducted from Tier I capital.

For purposes of calculating Tier I capital, the amount of MSR and PCCR that may be included cannot exceed the lesser of 90 percent of the asset's fair market value or 100 percent of their remaining book value, determined at least quarterly.

Capital Adequacy

An institution may continue to include in capital other identifiable intangibles (such as core deposits) if they were included in core capital prior to 1992. The FRB, however, is likely to ignore these grandfathered intangibles when evaluating an institution's application for new powers, activities, or offices.

Servicing Rights

Effective March 31, 1996, FFIEC directed banks and thrifts to use FAS 122, "Accounting for Mortgage Servicing Rights," for Call and Thrift Financial Reporting purposes. Because FAS 122 eliminated the accounting distinction between originated mortgage servicing rights (OMSRs) and PMSRs, the FFIEC released an interim rule which permits the capitalization of OMSRs and requires market rate-based treatment testing.

Under the interim rule, financial institutions are to report OMSRs together with PMSRs as intangible assets and treat the two servicing rights the same for regulatory capital purposes. When determining Tier I capital for risk-based and leverage capital purposes, the maximum permissible amount of both OMSRs and PMSRs should be "included in" (i.e., not deducted from) regulatory capital.

On August 1, 1997, the agencies proposed to amend their risk-based capital rules to increase the amount of mortgage-servicing assets ("MSAs") that can be treated as Tier I capital from 50 percent to 100 percent of Tier I capital. Consistent with the current rule, the limit would include purchased credit card relationships ("PCCR") which would remain subject to a sub-limit of no more than 25 percent of Tier I capital limit. The proposal also retains the 10 percent haircut on the fair value of MSAs and PCCRs in computing their Tier I capital eligibility. However, the proposal does not expand this favorable capital treatment to servicing assets related to nonmortgage financial assets and "other intangibles." Such assets would continue to be deducted from Tier I capital, as would MSAs and PCCRs in excess of the 100 percent (and 25 percent) limits.

Deferred Tax Assets

The agencies limit the amount of deferred tax assets that are recognized in computing an institution's regulatory capital.

Changes in generally accepted accounting principles resulting from the 1992 promulgation of FAS 109 increase the recognition of assets resulting from deferred income tax benefits on financial statements.

The agencies recognize some deferred tax assets without limit, namely those that can be realized from:

- Taxes paid in prior carryback years; and

- Future reversals of existing temporary differences.

The agencies, however, limit recognition of deferred tax assets, such as carryforwards, whose realization depends on future taxable income. Capital recognition of these deferred tax assets is limited to the smaller of:

- The amount the institution is projected to realize within one year of the most recent calendar quarter-end date, excluding tax carryforwards expected to be used and existing temporary differences; or

- 10 percent of Tier I capital, prior to the deduction of nonqualifying intangibles and deferred tax assets.

Any excess above this limit is deducted from Tier I capital and from total assets for purposes of calculating both the risk-based and leverage capital ratios.

On the page 57 is a simplified worksheet that can be used to calculate regulatory capital.

Risk-Weighted Assets

Introduction

An institution's total risk-weighted assets (less capital-related deductions) is the denominator for both its Tier I and its total risk-based capital ratios. Determining total risk-weighted assets requires both reductions in, and additions to, total assets as shown on the institution's books:

- On-balance sheet assets are adjusted by factors varying from 0 percent to 100 percent, depending on their credit profile.

- Off-balance sheet items are partially recognized, similarly adjusted for their credit profile, and added to total assets.

These calculations are explained below.

Risk Weights for Balance Sheet Assets

The adjustment of balance sheet assets requires multiplying each asset by a credit risk-weighting factor (as determined by regulation) of 0 percent, 20 percent, 50 percent, or 100 percent. The resulting products then are added together.

Capital Calculation
(Numerator)

Tier I:	Common Stock & Related Surplus
	Qualifying Perpetual Preferred Stock & Related Surplus
	Undivided Profits
	Minority Interest in Consolidated Subs
	Other
Less:	Goodwill & Disallowed Intangibles
	TOTAL TIER I = _____
Tier II:	Subordinate Debt*
	Intermediate Term (orig. mat. 5 yrs.)
	Preferred Stock*
	Subtotal_____ Limited to 50% of Total Tier I
	Perpetual Preferred Stock
	Allowance for Loan and Lease Losses (ALLL) (limited to 1.25%** of total risk-weighted assets)
	Other
	Subtotal_____
	TOTAL TIER II = _____
	Limited to 100% of Total Tier I
	TIER I + TIER II = _____
Less:	Investments in Unconsolidated Subsidiaries: _____
	TOTAL CAPITAL _____

* Subject to a cumulative discount by a fifth of the original amount in each of the last five years prior to maturity.

** Note that the excess ALLL is not deducted, but rather just is not "added back."

Note: All deductions from capital also are subtracted from total assets.

Category 1 (0 percent)

The following balance sheet assets receive a risk weighting of 0 percent:

1. Cash (domestic and foreign) held in the bank or in transit;
2. Balances due from, and claims on, Federal Reserve banks and central banks in other OECD countries;[1]
3. Claims on, or unconditional guarantees by, the U.S. government or its agencies or other OECD countries;
4. Local currency claims on non-OECD central governments and central banks, to the extent the bank has local currency central banks liabilities in that country;
5. Claims collateralized by cash on deposit in the financial institutions owed such claims or secured by OECD central government or U.S. government and agency securities or unconditional direct guarantees for which a positive collateral margin is maintained daily;
6. Gold bullion held in bank vaults, to the extent it is backed by gold bullion liabilities;
7. Federal Reserve Bank Stock; and
8. For savings associations only, assets guaranteed by the FDIC/RTC (on January 1, 1996, the FDIC assumed all RTC authority) or its successor, FSLIC Resolution Fund.

Category 2 (20 percent)

The following balance sheet assets receive a risk weighting of 20 percent:

1. All claims (long- and short-term) on, or guaranteed by, OECD domestic depository institutions or non-OECD depository institutions with a residual maturity of one year or less;
2. Cash items in the process of collection;
3. Secured portions of loans and other assets partially collateralized by securities issued or guaranteed by the U.S. government or its agencies, or other OECD central governments;

---

[1] "*OECD countries*" mean those countries that are full members of the Organization of Economic Cooperation and Development, as well as those countries that have concluded special lending arrangements with the International Monetary Fund, but excludes any country that has rescheduled its external sovereign debt within the last five (5) years.

4. Portions of loans and other assets collateralized by cash on deposit in the lending institution;

5. Portions of loans and other assets conditionally guaranteed by the U.S. government or its agencies, or other OECD central governments;

6. Securities and other claims on, or guaranteed by, U.S. government-sponsored agencies;

7. Portions of loans and other assets collateralized by securities issued by, or guaranteed by, U.S. government-sponsored agencies;

8. Claims of or general obligations of, and portions of claims guaranteed by, public sector entities in OECD countries, below the level of central government;

9. Claims on or guaranteed by official multilateral lending institutions or regional development institutions in which the U.S. government is a shareholder or a contributing member;

10. Portions of loans and other assets collateralized with securities issued by official multilateral lending institutions or regional development institutions in which the U.S. government is a shareholder or a contributing member; and

11. For banks and bank holding companies only, assets subject to guarantee by the FDIC/RTC (with some exceptions).

Category 3 (50 percent)

The following balance sheet assets receive a risk weighting of 50 percent:

1. Assets secured by a first mortgage on a one- to four-family residential property that are not more than 90 days past due, on nonaccrual, or restructured, and certain privately issued mortgage-backed securities representing indirect ownership of such loans;

2. Credit equivalent amounts of interest rate and exchange rate-related contracts, except for those assigned to a lower risk category;

3. Revenue bonds or similar obligations, including loans and leases, that are obligations of public sector entities in OECD countries, but for which the government entity is committed to repay the debt only out of revenues from the facilities financed;

4. Certain multifamily residential mortgages; and

5. Certain loans for the construction of presold one- to four-family residences.

Category 4 (100 percent)

The following balance sheet items receive a risk weighting of 100 percent:

1. All other claims on private obligors;

2. Claims on non-OECD financial institutions with an original maturity exceeding one year (claims on non-OECD central banks with a residual maturity exceeding one year are included in this category unless they qualify for item 4 of Category 1);

3. Claims on non-OECD central governments that are not included in item 4 of Category 1;

4. Obligations issued by state or local governments repayable solely by a private party or enterprise;

5. Fixed assets, other real estate owned, and all other assets including claims on commercial firms owned by the public sector;

6. Investments in unconsolidated subsidiaries, joint ventures, or associated companies (unless deducted from capital and assets);

7. Capital instruments issued by other banking organizations;

8. Assets sold with recourse, with certain exceptions as provided for in the call report instructions;

9. Single family residential mortgages that do not qualify for a 50 percent risk weight; and

10. Deferred tax assets not included for regulatory capital.

Mutual Funds

Banks and bank holding companies must risk-weight their mutual fund holdings at the weight of the highest risk asset permitted in the fund's operating rules. **Savings associations** should risk-weight their mutual fund holdings at the weight applicable to the "riskiest" asset actually held by the fund at the reporting date.

Assets Sold with Recourse

The regulatory agencies recognize only a few types of asset sales with recourse (notably those to government agencies and some asset sales using spread accounts as a limited recourse mechanism) as removing the asset from the balance sheet for capital calculation purposes. Other assets sold with recourse remain on the balance sheet in their entirety. This treatment is consistent with the Basle guidelines.

Capital Adequacy

While the agencies' current rules differ slightly in how the volume of risk assets sold with limited recourse are quantified, in substance, they permit institutions to count the lesser of:

- The minimum risk-based capital required to support the assets as if not sold; or

- The actual recourse amount.

On November 5, 1997, the agencies jointly proposed to modify the risk-based capital rules to address other recourse arrangements and direct credit substitutes (collectively defined as "positions") associated with asset securitizations. The agencies proposed to:

- Formalize their focus on the economic substance of positions in determining appropriate risk-based capital treatment;

- Recognize different levels of concentrated credit risk associated with such positions;

- Require minimum regulatory capital to be held on a scaled basis against them; and

- Provide some relative risk-weight relief for investment grade positions, the status of which would be determined through one or more mechanisms, such as a continuous public rating scheme, a ratings benchmark approach, and/or a historic loss/internal risk assessment methodology.

Credit Conversion of and Risk Weights for Off-Balance Sheet Assets

To assess the risk weights for off-balance sheet items, federal regulators use a two-step process. First, the principal or face value amount of the off-balance sheet item is multiplied by a credit conversion factor to derive a balance sheet "credit equivalent amount." Then the credit equivalent amount is adjusted by the appropriate credit risk factor based on the obligor, the guarantor, or the type of collateral.

100 Percent Conversion Factor

1. Direct credit substitutes (i.e., any irrevocable off-balance sheet obligation in which a bank has essentially the same credit risk as if it made a direct loan to the obligor). Examples are:

a. Guarantees or guarantee-type instruments backing financial claims such as outstanding securities claims such as outstanding securities, loans, and other financial liabilities;

b. Standby letters of credit; and

c. Surety arrangements that back or guarantee repayment of commercial paper, tax-exempt securities, and commercial or individual loans or debt obligations.

2. Acquisitions of risk participations in bankers' acceptances and participations in direct credit substitutes;

3. Sale and repurchase agreements and asset sales with recourse, if not already included on the balance sheet for regulatory reporting purposes; and

4. Forward agreements (forward purchases, forward deposits accepted, and partly paid shares and securities) to purchase assets.

50 Percent Conversion Factor

1. Transaction-related contingencies (e.g., standby letters of credit that serve as bid and performance bonds and warranties);

2. Unused commitments with an original maturity exceeding one year (commercial and consumer credit commitments); and

3. Revolving underwriting facilities (RUFs) and note issuance facilities (NIFs) where a borrower can issue short-term paper in its own name on a revolving basis and the underwriting banks have a legally binding commitment to either purchase any notes the borrower is unable to sell by the rollover date or to advance funds to the borrower.

20 Percent Conversion Factor

Short-term, self-liquidating, trade-related contingencies that arise from the movement of goods. This includes commercial letters of credit and other documentary letters of credit collateralized by the underlying shipments.

0 Percent Conversion Factor

Unused commitments with an original maturity of one year or less or that are unconditionally cancellable at any time. Unused retail credit card lines are included if the bank has the unconditional option to cancel the card at any time. So too are unused home equity lines of credit that are subject to annual receipt and review of appropriate financial information and renewal.

Capital Adequacy

Interest Rate, Foreign Exchange Rate, and Commodity Contracts

Total risk-weighted assets must include a credit equivalent amount for the following off-balance sheet interest rate and foreign exchange rate instruments:

Interest Rate-Related Contracts

1. Single currency interest rate swaps;
2. Basis swaps;
3. Forward rate agreements;
4. Interest rate options purchased; and
5. Any other instrument that gives rise to similar credit risk.

Exchange Rate-Related Contracts

1. Cross-currency interest rate swaps;
2. Forward foreign exchange contracts;
3. Currency options purchased; and
4. Any other instrument that gives rise to similar credit risk.

Commodity-Related or Equity Derivative-Related Contracts

1. Commodity-linked or equity-linked swaps;
2. Commodity-linked or equity-linked options purchased;
3. Forward commodity-linked or equity-linked contracts; and
4. Any other instrument linked to commodities or equities that give rise to similar credit risks.

Exclusions

Foreign exchange rate contracts with original maturities of 14 or fewer calendar days and exchange-traded derivative contracts subject to daily cash margin requirements may be excluded from the capital adequacy calculations. Although gold contracts are generally accorded the same treatment applied to foreign exchange contracts for capital calculation purposes, the 14 or fewer calendar day original maturity exclusion does not apply to gold contracts, all of which must be included irrespective of original maturity.

Conversion Factors Determining the "Add-On" Values of OTC Derivative Contracts					
Remaining Maturity	Interest Rate	FX & Gold	Equity	Precious Metals (except gold)	Other Commodities
One year or less	0.0%	1.0%	6.0%	7.0%	10.0%
Over one year to five years	0.5%	5.0%	8.0%	7.0%	12.0%
More than five years	1.5%	7.5%	10.0%	8.0%	15.0%

Netting

Institutions are permitted to net positive and negative market values of rate contracts subject to a qualifying legally enforceable bilateral netting arrangement with a counterparty. These qualifying master arrangements create a single legal obligation covering all included individual rate contracts and do not contain walkaway clauses. A walkaway clause permits a nondefaulting counterparty to make no or lower payments than otherwise contracted to a defaulter or the defaulter's estate even if the defaulter, or its estate, is a net creditor under the contract. Prescribed legal opinions or memoranda of law concluding on the netting contracts' enforceability in all the relevant jurisdictions are required.

Calculation of Credit Equivalent Amounts

Federal agencies require that institutions subject to the U.S. risk-based capital rules follow the **current exposure method** of measuring exposure to certain derivative contracts, including foreign exchange, interest rate, equity, precious metals, and other commodities contracts. The credit equivalent amount of the off-balance sheet instruments is calculated by summing:

- The mark-to-market value of the contract; and

- An estimate (the "add-on") of the potential increase in credit exposure over the remaining life of all such contracts by multiplying the face value of all contracts by the conversion factors.

The potential future credit exposure on a contract not subject to a qualifying bilateral netting agreement is calculated by multiplying the principal amount of the contract by one of the following credit conversion factors:

As the preceding table reflects, the credit conversion factors increase as the remaining contract maturity lengthens. For most contracts the remaining maturity is the term to final maturity. Contracts structured to periodically settle outstanding exposure on specified dates, when the terms are reset such that the contract's market value is zero on those dates, represent an exception. For these contracts, the remaining maturity for conversion factor purposes is the term to the next reset date. However, interest rate contracts with remaining maturities over one year that meet this criterion are subject to a minimum conversion factor of 0.5 percent.

Conversion factors applicable to contracts with multiple exchanges of principal are to be multiplied by the number of remaining principal payments. Finally, derivative contracts not explicitly covered by the conversion table are to be treated as "other commodities."

No potential credit exposure is calculated for single currency interest rate swaps in which payments are based upon two floating rate indices (so called floating/floating or basis swaps). Their credit exposure is evaluated solely on a mark-to-market basis.

The credit equivalent(s) amount of derivative contracts that are subject to a qualifying bilateral netting contract(s) is calculated by adding the net current exposure of the netting contract and the sum of the estimates of potential future exposure for all individual contracts subject to the netting contract, adjusted to take into account the effects of the netting contract. The net current exposure is the sum of all positive and negative mark-to-market values of the individual contracts subject to the netting agreement. If the net sum of the mark-to-market values is positive, then the net current exposure is equal to that sum. If the net sum of the mark-to-market values is zero or negative, then the net current exposure is zero. The impact of a bilateral netting agreement on the gross potential future exposure associated with derivative contracts with a particular counterparty is recognized through the application of the following formula, which results in an adjusted add-on amount (Anet). The formula employs the ratio of net current exposure to gross current exposure (NGR) and is expressed as:

Anet = (0.4 x Agross) + 0.6(NGR x Agross)

The ratio NGR is to be determined by consistently using either the counterparty-by-counterparty approach or the aggregate approach. The aggregate approach establishes an overall or average NGR which is used in each application of the formula to the respective gross exposures associated with a particular bilateral netting agreement. The counterparty-by-counterparty approach establishes an NGR for each bilateral contract. Net negative mark-to-market values to individual counterparties cannot be used to offset net positive current exposures to other counterparties. Also, in calculating potential future credit exposure for contracts in which notional principal is equivalent to cash flows, total notional principal is defined as the net receipts to each party falling due on each value date in each currency.

Finally, to avoid double counting, any on-balance sheet assets which fully or partially reflect off-balance sheet activities covered by the risk-based capital rules are to be excluded from the balance sheet assets used in calculating the risk-based capital ratios.

Risk Weights for Interest Rate, Foreign Exchange, and Commodity Contracts

Once the credit equivalent amount for interest and exchange rates has been determined, that amount will be weighted within the overall framework according to the category of the counterparty and the nature of any underlying collateral or guarantees. Such enhancements may also be considered in risk weighting credit equivalent amounts derived under qualifying master bilateral netting arrangements, so long as the enhancements are available against all rate contracts covered by the netting arrangement. The maximum credit equivalent applicable to foreign exchange and interest rate swaps is 50 percent.

In those cases where the credit exposure on interest rate and foreign exchange rate contracts already is reflected on the balance sheet, counter party exposures will be deducted from balance sheet assets when calculating the risk-weighted asset figure to avoid double counting.

Interest Rate Risk

> The regulatory agencies are becoming more uniform in their consideration of interest rate risk.

The banking and thrift regulators deal somewhat differently with interest rate risk (IRR).

The banking agencies have opted to evaluate the impact of IRR on capital adequacy on an institution specific basis within the broader context of the "risk assessment" examination approach. The supervisors require additional reporting for institutions with "excessive" exposure to IRR. Institutions deemed to be low risk are exempt from these reporting requirements. For those institutions required to report on their IRR, the supervisors will appraise the bank's controls and test the bank's own internal models for measuring IRR.

This approach relies on a bank's internal measures of risk, evaluation of the adequacy of the bank's risk management process, and use of supervisory

Capital Adequacy 67

screens, including a standardized interest rate risk model. Banks that are found to have high levels of exposure to interest rate risk (in terms of earnings and the economic value of equity) will be subject to supervisory directives that could include such actions as raising additional capital, strengthening rate risk management expertise, improving management information and measurement systems, and reducing exposure levels.

The OTS requires savings associations to report information on their interest rate risk profile. The information is used in OTS's Market Valuation Model to estimate the change in their lending portfolio market value under various interest rate scenarios. A savings association must deduct from regulatory capital half of the estimated decline in its net portfolio value resulting from a 200 basis point change in market interest rates in excess of 2 percent of the estimated economic value of its total assets.

The OTS issued a proposed Thrift Bulletin in April 1998, notifying the industry of changes in the agency's review of interest rate risk. The OTS proposes to allow large institution's $1 billion in assets to use their own IRR model to evaluate their risk. Small institutions may continue to use the calculations they perform quarterly in producing their reports to the OTS.

Market Risk Rule

In accordance with the December 1995 market risk amendment to the Basle Committee capital framework, the U.S. banking agencies revised their risk-based capital rules on September 9, 1996, to address market risk. The amendment requires banks and bank holding companies with significant trading activities to measure and hold capital for exposure to:

- General market risk, defined as changes in the market value of on-balance sheet assets and off-balance sheet items resulting from fluctuations in interest rates, equity prices, foreign exchange, and commodity prices; and

- Specific risk, defined as changes in the market value of individual positions due to factors other than broad market movements such as idiosyncratic variations, event risk, and default risk.

More particularly, as of January 1, 1998, institutions with significant market risk must:

- Maintain regulatory capital on a daily basis at an overall minimum 8.0 percent ratio of total qualifying capital to risk-weighted assets, adjusted for market risk;

- Include a supplemental market risk capital charge in their risk-based capital calculations and quarterly regulatory financial reports; and

- Maintain appropriate internal measurement, reporting, and risk management systems to generate and monitor the basis for the value-at-risk (VAR) and the associated market risk capital charge.

The internal model(s) and supporting systems are to be subject to periodic internal and external audits and backtesting. Backtesting requirements will apply one year after an institution begins its compliance with the final guideline.

The market risk capital requirement applies to banks and bank holding companies (BHC) with trading activities amounting to $1 billion or more or to 10 percent or more of total assets, and to other institutions on a case-by-case basis. Trading activities are defined as the sum of trading assets and trading liabilities as reported in an institution's most recent consolidated call report or BHC Y-9C Report. The agencies may exempt institutions from the requirement, consistent with safety and soundness considerations.

A bank or BHC that must comply with the market risk capital amendment will treat the quarterly calculation of its total risk-based capital ratio adjusted for market risk as the total risk-based capital ratio for capital adequacy, prompt corrective action, and other statutory and regulatory purposes. Higher minimum capital levels may be mandated by an institution's regulator for safety and soundness considerations, such as concerns regarding the level and direction of market risk exposure, and the adequacy of risk measurement and management systems.

The additional regulatory reporting and supplemental capital charge are to capture an institution's general market risk of on-balance sheet and off-balance sheet foreign exchange and commodity positions and the general and specific market risks associated with the trading of debt and equity instruments. Debt, equity, and commodity positions included in the market risk measure (except for over-the-counter ("OTC") derivatives) are to be excluded from the credit risk capital calculation. Foreign exchange positions outside the trading account and OTC derivatives are to be included in *both* the market risk and credit risk capital calculations. With primary regulator concurrence, banks and BHCs may use internal models to calculate general market and, as possible, certain specific risk exposures. These models must satisfy certain quantitative and qualitative supervisory criteria.

The most recent capital rules introduce a unique category of regulatory capital. Called "Tier III" capital, it is available for only one purpose: to cover market risk that is not adequately covered by qualifying Tier I and Tier II capital. Tier III capital consists of short-term subordinated debt with an original maturity of at least two years. This debt must be unsecured and not yet fully advanced, and must not be redeemable prior to maturity if the institution is or will be upon redemption less than adequately capitalized, unless issuer's banking supervisor gives prior approval. Tier III capital may not exceed 250 percent of Tier I capital.

The mechanics of the modified total risk-based capital ratio include adjustments to both the numerator, as described above, and to the denominator. The denominator is the adjusted capital component risk-weighted assets plus market risk-equivalent assets. As mentioned earlier, risk-weighted assets determined through the application of the credit risk-based capital standards are reduced by the risk-weighted amounts of all positions covered by the market risk measure, except for OTC derivatives and foreign exchange transactions outside of the trading account. An institution's market risk-equivalent assets equal the capital charge for market risk multiplied by 12.5 (the reciprocal of 8.0 percent minimum capital requirement). The market risk capital charge is the larger of either the average VAR measured for the last 60 business days and increased by a supervisory assigned multiplication factor of not less than three, or the previous day's VAR calculation (not subject to the multiplication factor). The multiplication factor is three unless backtesting results indicate that a higher factor is appropriate or as the institution's banking agency may otherwise determine.

Minimum Leverage Ratio Requirement

Introduction and Purpose

All of the regulatory agencies augment the risk-based capital standards by requiring a minimum leverage-based capital ratio. This "leverage ratio" is a minimum ratio of core capital expressed as a percentage of average total on-balance sheet assets, adjusted for deductions from regulatory capital.

The purpose of the minimum leverage ratio is to provide a base level of capital to protect against interest rate, liquidity, operational, and concentration risks that are not measured by the risk-based capital ratio.

Agency Requirements

The leverage requirement applies differently to different types of institutions:

- **For banks and bank holding companies.** The most highly rated banks in terms of safe and sound operations (i.e., those rated a composite "1" under the CAMELS system used by the OCC, FDIC, and FRB) are required to meet a minimum Tier I leverage capital ratio equaling at least 3 percent of adjusted total assets. All other banks are required to meet a minimum of at least 100 to 200 basis points above the 3 percent level. A bank's leverage ratio is calculated by dividing its Tier I capital by its average total on-balance sheet assets, adjusted for any core capital deductions.

- **For savings associations.** The OTS requires savings associations to maintain core capital equaling at least 3 percent of total assets. The OTS is proposing to revise its requirement to be at least as stringent as the OCC's requirements for national banks.

Savings associations must meet a third capital ratio called the "tangible capital requirement." Under this requirement, a savings association must maintain tangible capital in an amount at least equal to 1.5 percent of the institution's adjusted total assets. **Tangible capital** is defined as core capital less supervisory goodwill and a portion of purchased mortgage servicing rights.

Prompt Corrective Action Categories

Introduction

Regulators must take prompt corrective action against an insured bank or thrift when the institution becomes less than adequately capitalized. Under joint regulations, the regulators (a) define the five capital categories and (b) specify how an institution determines its own category.

The prompt corrective action regulations apply only to insured banks and thrifts, not to their holding companies. A holding company, however, must guarantee any capital plan submitted by one of its undercapitalized subsidiaries.

The Five Capital Categories

Supervisory sanctions are based on the capital level of a financial institution. There are five capital categories, each of which is determined by reference to three different capital ratios:

- Total risk-based capital;

- Tier I risk-based capital; and

- Total leverage capital.

Capital Adequacy 71

PCA Capital Categories	Total Risk-Based Ratio	Tier I Risk-Based Ratio	Leverage Ratio
Well Capitalized	≥ 10%	≥ 6%	≥ 5%
Adequately Capitalized	≥ 8%	≥ 4%	≥ 4%*
Undercapitalized	< 8%	< 4%	< 4%*
Significantly Undercapitalized	<6%	< 3%	< 3%
Critically Undercapitalized	Tangible equity ≤ 2.0 percent **		

* 3.0 for 1-rated banks.

** The tangible equity ratio is defined as: (a) Tier I capital plus cumulative preferred stock and related surplus, less intangibles (except qualifying purchased mortgage-servicing rights (PMSR)); divided by (b) total assets, less intangibles (except qualifying PMSR).

The minimum ratios for each capital category are shown in the above chart.

Mandated Corrective Actions

Well Capitalized

Only the well capitalized institutions are insulated from regulatory restrictions. And even these institutions are forbidden from paying dividends or other capital distributions that would create an undercapitalized institution.

Adequately Capitalized

An adequately capitalized institution (i.e., one that meets all regulatory minimums) may not accept brokered or high-rate deposits without the FDIC's approval. FDIC's approval is also needed to insure the deposits of participants in an employee benefit plan separately on a pass-through basis.

An adequately capitalized institution also runs a significant risk of a regulatory action demoting it to an undercapitalized institution.

Undercapitalized

An undercapitalized or a significantly undercapitalized institution must file a capital restoration plan with its regulator. A capital restoration plan must show not only how the institution will raise capital, but also how it will preserve capital by limiting asset growth and geographic and product expansion. The institution may not pay dividends or other capital distribution and it may not accept brokered or high-rate deposits. The regulator has 60 days to approve or reject the plan and must send a copy of any approved plan to the FDIC.

If the institution filing the capital plan is a subsidiary of a holding company, the plan will not be approved unless the holding company partially guarantees the institution's performance. This guarantee nominally is limited to the smaller of (i) 5 percent of the institution's assets when it became undercapitalized, or (ii) the amount necessary to achieve capital compliance when the institution fails to meet its capital plan. The agency may overcome the nominal limit through successive demands for new capital plans.

This holding company guarantee is in addition to any preexisting holding company obligations under a net worth maintenance or similar agreement. The guarantee expires when the subsidiary has been adequately capitalized on average for each of four consecutive calendar quarters.

Significantly Undercapitalized

A significantly undercapitalized institution, or any institution that fails to establish and comply with an approved capital plan, is subject to further rigorous measures. A regulator might, for example, replace officers or directors, order new capital to be sold (even at a diluted price), or impose a supervisory merger. Other possible sanctions include bans on accepting deposits from other banks or on bank holding company dividends. Failure to submit or comply with a capital plan also may lead to the appointment of a conservator or receiver, even if the institution has positive net worth.

Critically Undercapitalized

An institution is critically undercapitalized if its tangible capital is less than 2 percent of its total assets. Critically undercapitalized institutions typically will be placed in receivership within 90 days.

Determining a Bank or Thrift Capital Category

A bank or thrift determines its own capital category by:

1. Computing its capital ratios as of the required filing date of its recent call report;

Capital Adequacy

2. Receiving an examination report indicating its capital category; or

3. Receiving a regulatory notice designating a different capital category.

A regulator may rely on one of three predicates to notify a bank or thrift of a different capital ratio:

1. A report the bank or thrift itself must file with its regulator within 15 days after an event significant enough to lower its capital category;

2. A finding of unsafe or unsound banking practices after a formal administrative hearing; or

3. A regulatory examiner's rating of "less than satisfactory" for the institution's asset quality, management, earnings, or liquidity.

None of these predicates automatically affects a bank's capital ratio; they merely supply the basis for an agency notice. The bank or thrift usually is given 14 or more days to challenge the notice of a new capital category. It may submit written evidence or arguments to support its challenge, and in some instances may request an informal hearing.

"Well-Capitalized" Bank Holding Companies

These prompt corrective action standards do not apply to a bank holding company. The Federal Reserve Board, however, does employ a definition of "well-capitalized" in its regulation of bank holding companies.

A bank holding company is "well-capitalized" if:

- On a consolidated basis, its total risk-weighted capital ratio is 10 percent or greater;

- On a consolidated basis, its Tier I risk-weighted capital ratio is 6 percent or greater; and

- The Federal Reserve Board has not directed the BHC to maintain any specific capital level.

A BHC that is both "well capitalized" and "well managed" will receive expedited processing of notices or applications to acquire additional banks or to engage in additional activities.

References

Laws:

12 U.S.C. 3907

Regulations:

12 CFR Part 3 (OCC)
12 CFR Part 6 (OCC)
12 CFR Part 208, Appendix A and B (FRB)
12 CFR Part 225, Appendix A, B, and D (FRB)
12 CFR Part 325 (FDIC)
12 CFR Part 567 (OTS)

X. Daylight Overdrafts

Introduction and Purpose 76

Covered Institutions 76

Daylight Overdrafts 76

Net Debit Caps 76

Self-Assessment Cap 77

Cap Multiples 78

De Minimis Cap 78

Zero Cap 79

Overdraft Administration 79

Overdraft Pricing 79

Foreign Banks 80

References 80

Introduction and Purpose

The Federal Reserve Board has issued guidelines in the form of a Policy Statement to address intraday risks in the payment system. Payment system risk can arise from transactions on the Federal Reserve's wire transfer system (Fedwire), from other types of payments, including checks and automated clearinghouse (ACH) transactions, and from transactions on private large-dollar networks. Risk is inherent in any system that permits participants to transmit payment messages throughout the day and settle their net positions at the end of the day.

The FRB's Policy Statement is intended, in part, to reduce the direct risk to the Federal Reserve System should a depository institution be unable to settle, before the end of the day, the intraday ("daylight") overdrafts in its Federal Reserve account. The Policy Statement also is concerned about the systemic or indirect risks to the Federal Reserve System if an institution participating in a large-dollar payments network is unable or unwilling to settle its net debit position.

This section of the *Handbook* addresses that portion of the Federal Reserve's requirements that govern daylight overdrafts in Federal Reserve accounts.

Covered Institutions

The FRB's Policy Statement applies to all FDIC-insured depository institutions and to all U.S. branches and agencies of foreign banks ("depository institutions").

Daylight Overdrafts

A daylight overdraft occurs when a depository institution's Federal Reserve account is in a negative position during the business day.

Net Debit Caps

To limit the aggregate amount of daylight credit extended by Reserve Banks, each institution that incurs more than *de minimis* daylight overdrafts in its Federal Reserve account must adopt a net debit cap. A net debit cap is a ceiling on the aggregate net debit position that an institution can incur (i) during a two-week period and (ii) on any single day. Each bank or savings association must notify its Federal Reserve Bank annually of its net debit cap.

Daylight Overdrafts

Alternatively, if an institution's daylight overdrafts generally do not exceed the lesser of $10 million or 20 percent of capital, the institution may qualify for exempt-from-filing status.

The net debit caps are based on a multiple of the institution's total risk-based capital. The multiple varies dependent on the institution's cap category. For most large institutions, a cap category of high, above average, or average is determined by the institution itself through a self-assessment process.

Self-Assessment Cap

An institution that wishes to establish a net debit cap category of high, above average, or average must perform an annual self-assessment of its own creditworthiness, intraday funds management and controls, customer credit policies and controls, operating controls, and contingency procedures.

To assist a bank in assessing its own creditworthiness, the Federal Reserve has adopted a simplified method based on the bank's supervisory rating and prompt corrective action (PCA) capital category. The supervisory rating and the PCA capital category are combined into a single rating for the creditworthiness component of the self-assessment using the creditworthiness matrix shown below:

Capital Level	Supervisory Composite Rating		
	Strong	**Satisfactory**	**Fair**
Well-Capitalized	Excellent	Very Good	Adequate
Adequately Capitalized	Very Good	Very Good	Adequate
Undercapitalized	*	*	Below Standard

* Institutions that fall into this category should perform a full assessment of creditworthiness.

An institution performing a self-assessment must also assess its procedures for evaluating the financial condition of its customers and should establish intraday credit limits that reflect these assessments. Finally, an institution should ensure that its operational controls and contingency procedures are sufficient to prevent losses due to fraud or system failures.

The Guide to the Federal Reserve's Payments Systems Risk Policy, available from any district Federal Reserve Bank, includes a detailed explanation of the steps that an institution should take in performing a self-assessment to establish a net debit cap.

The self-assessment and cap category selection process should be reviewed at least once in each 12-month period by an institution's board of directors.

Cap Multiples

Net debit caps resulting from the self-assessment are expressed as multiples of capital as listed below:

Net Debit Cap Multiples		
Category	Two-Week Avg.	Single Day
High	1.50	2.25
Above Average	1.125	1.875
Average	0.75	1.125
De Minimis	0.40	0.40
Exempt from Filing	$10 million	
	$10 million	
Zero	0.0	0.0

***De Minimis* Cap**

Many depository institutions incur relatively small overdrafts and thus pose little risk to the Federal Reserve. To ease the burden of the self-assessment process and to ease Federal Reserve's administering caps, the Fed allows institutions that meet reasonable safety standards to incur *de minimis* amounts of daylight overdrafts up to 40 percent of capital without performing a self-assessment.

The Reserve Bank will review the status of an exempt institution that incurs overdrafts in its Federal Reserve account in excess of $10 million or 20 percent of capital on more than two days in any two rolling two-week reserve-maintenance periods. The Federal Reserve will decide whether to maintain the exemption or to require the institution to file for a cap. Even for institutions meeting the size and frequency standards, the Federal Reserve has discretion to grant or deny the exemption.

An institution choosing to use a *de minimis* cap must submit to its Reserve Bank, at least once each year, a copy of the resolution of its board of directors approving the bank's use of daylight credit up to the *de minimis* level.

The net debit cap provisions of this policy apply to foreign banks to the same extent as they apply to U.S. institutions.

The Reserve Banks will advise home country supervisors of banks with U.S. branches and agencies of the daylight overdraft capacity of banks under their jurisdiction, as well as of other pertinent conditions related to their caps.

Zero Cap

A depository institution may have a cap of zero imposed by its Reserve Bank because of the institution's troubled status, because of FRB policy (such as limited purpose trust companies), or because the institution itself requested a zero cap.

Overdraft Administration

An institution is expected to avoid incurring net debits that, on average over a two-week period, exceed the two-week average cap *and*, on any day, exceed the single-day cap. The two-week average cap provides flexibility in recognition that fluctuations in payments can occur from day to day.

The purpose of the higher single-day cap is to limit excessive daylight overdrafts on any day and to ensure that institutions develop internal controls that focus on the exposures each day, as well as over time.

Under certain circumstances, the Federal Reserve may prohibit the use of Federal Reserve intraday credit if:

1. An institution's use of daylight credit is deemed by the institution's supervisor to be unsafe or unsound;

2. An institution does not qualify for a cap exemption, does not perform a self-assessment, or does not file a board of directors-approved *de minimis* cap; and

3. An institution poses an excessive risk to a Reserve Bank.

Overdraft Pricing

On April 14, 1994, the Federal Reserve began charging a fee for average daily intraday overdrafts in reserve clearing accounts. As of April 13, 1995, the fee is 36 basis points (annual rate), quoted on the basis of a 24-hour day. For a 10-hour Fedwire operating day, the fee would be 15 basis points. In 1997, the Federal Reserve decided to maintain the fee at the 36-basis-point level.

The fee applies to average daily combined funds and book-entry securities intraday overdrafts in accounts at the Federal Reserve. The average daily overdraft is calculated by dividing the sum of the negative reserve or clearing account balances at the end of each minute by the total number of minutes in a Fedwire operating day.

To provide a *de minimis* level of free overdrafts, Reserve Banks will deduct from the gross fee for average overdrafts an amount equal to 10 percent of qualifying capital. Fees of $25 or less in any two-week interval will be waived. Because the fee applicable to the deductible is kept constant at the 10-hour-operating-day rate, any changes to the scheduled Fedwire operating day will not affect the value of the deductible.

The pricing deductible is independent of the exempt-from-filing test under the net-debit-cap policy. An institution could be exempt from filing for a cap but be subject to pricing because its average overdrafts were over 10 percent of its capital. It could also have to file for a cap because its peak overdrafts exceeded the lesser of 20 percent of its capital or $10 million, but be exempt from pricing because its average overdrafts were less than 10 percent of its capital.

Foreign Banks

A foreign bank whose home country supervisor adheres to the Basle Capital Accord may determine its uncollateralized daylight overdraft capacity by applying its cap multiple to the greater of 10 percent of worldwide capital or 5 percent of the total liabilities of each agency or branch, including acceptances, but excluding accrued expenses and liabilities due to other offices and affiliates.

All foreign banks may incur total overdrafts up to an amount equal to their cap multiple times 10 percent of their worldwide capital, as long as the amount of the overdraft above the uncollateralized cap is collateralized. In addition, all foreign banks may elect to collateralize all or a portion of their overdrafts related to book-entry securities activity.

Annual daylight overdraft capital for foreign banks is reported on Form FR 2225 and filed with the district Federal Reserve Bank.

References

Federal Reserve Policy Statement on Payments System Risk, effective December 8, 1997.

XI. Dividends

Introduction and Purpose 82

Limitations for Banks 82

Two-Part Test 82

Capital Limitations Test 12 U.S.C. 56 82

"Surplus Surplus" Transfers 83

Earnings Limitation Test 12 U.S.C. 60 83

Limitations for Savings Associations 84

OTS Dividend Regulations 84

OTS Tier Levels 84

OTS Tier 1 Dividends 84

OTS Tier 2 Dividends 85

OTS Tier 3 Dividends 85

OTS Supervision Restrictions 85

Future OTS Revision 86

References 86

Introduction and Purpose

Generally, the authority of a bank or savings association to pay dividends is limited by both income and capital measures. National banks' and state member banks' dividend payments are governed by 12 U.S.C. 56 and 60. These two complementary sections are intended to:

- Protect against capital impairment by requiring that the dividend paying bank has sufficient capital (12 U.S.C. 56); and

- Limit the payment of dividends to ensure that they are not in excess of the bank's recent earnings (12 U.S.C. 60).

State banks are subject to the dividend provisions in the state in which they are chartered. Provisions of state law often are modeled after federal requirements. State member banks are subject to the more restrictive of the state or federal provisions.

Savings associations are subject to the dividend restrictions mandated by FIRREA and applicable OTS regulations that sharply differ from those applicable to banks.

Under FDICIA, no insured institution may pay a dividend or make any other capital distribution if after that distribution the institution would be undercapitalized.

Limitations for Banks

Two-Part Test

For national and state member banks, both the capital impairment standard of Section 56 and the earnings standard of Section 60 must be satisfied before a bank may declare a dividend.

Capital Limitations Test 12 U.S.C. 56

The first part of the dividends test is the "capital limitations test." Section 56 and implementing regulations provide three major limitations on dividend payment:

- No bank may withdraw any part of its capital;

- No dividend may be paid if losses have been sustained that equal or exceed "undivided profits then on hand"; and

- No dividend may be paid in excess of "undivided profits."

In the past, the undivided profit measures employed allowed banks to increase allowable dividends by adding back the allowance for loan and lease losses ("ALLL"). Current regulations forbid this practice after January 1, 1991.

For state member banks, the Federal Reserve's rules apply to dividends on both preferred stock and common stock in its definition of "dividends." In contrast, for national banks, the OCC's rules apply only to common stock dividends.

"Surplus Surplus" Transfers

To the extent a bank's surplus fund exceeds its common capital, this amount, known as "surplus surplus," may be transferred to the net profits accounts and made available for payment of dividends provided that:

- The "surplus surplus" actually represents earnings and not paid-in contributions;

- The bank's board of directors approves the transfer; and

- The transfer is approved by the Federal Reserve for state member banks or the OCC for national banks. In 1996, the OCC eliminated this requirement for national banks.

Earnings Limitation Test 12 U.S.C. 60

The second part of the dividends test is the **"earnings limitation test."** Section 60 limits the payment of dividends based upon the bank's recent earnings. To comply with the limitations of Section 60, a bank seeking to declare a dividend must comply with the following standards:

- Until the surplus account equals the common stock account, at least one-tenth of net income of the preceding half year in the case of quarterly or semiannual dividends (or two consecutive half-year periods in the case of annual dividends) must be carried to the surplus account; and

- OCC or Federal Reserve approval is required if dividends exceed the total of the bank's net income combined with its retained net income of the preceding two years, less required transfers to surplus or a fund for retirement of preferred stock.

When computing undivided profits, it is no longer permissible to add ALLL provisions to net profits or subtract net write-offs.

Limitations for Savings Associations

OTS Dividend Regulations

Current OTS regulations restrict a savings association's distributions of earnings and capital based on the capital adequacy of the institution. OTS expects that these regulations will be replaced with language similar to that of a proposed rule which is discussed at the end of this section.

OTS Tier Levels

For the purpose of determining allowable dividends, OTS segregates savings associations into three major categories, or Tiers:

- A Tier 1 savings association is one that meets current capital requirements after giving effect to the proposed dividend;

- A Tier 2 savings association is one that only meets minimum capital requirements after giving effect to its proposed dividend; and

- A Tier 3 savings association is one that fails to meet capital requirements after giving effect to the proposed dividend.

Though many savings association dividends do not require OTS approval, a savings association must notify OTS at least 30 days before making any dividend payment. The notification must be in writing and provided to the savings association's district director.

OTS Tier 1 Dividends

Given their higher capital, Tier 1 savings associations have the most liberal dividend distribution authority.

- Without approval, a Tier 1 savings association may distribute up to 100 percent of its net income earned during that calendar year.

- Also without approval, a Tier 1 savings association may distribute up to one-half of its "surplus" capital, if at the beginning of the year the savings association exceeded current capital requirements.

- Additionally, OTS may approve distributions in excess of these provisions so long as the distributions are consistent with safe and sound operation of the savings association.

OTS Tier 2 Dividends

Tier 2 savings associations may less liberally declare and pay dividends. Limits are set by capital requirements that were phased in during 1991 and 1993.

- If the Tier 2 savings association fails to meet its current capital requirements, but satisfies its January 1, 1993, requirements, it may distribute up to 75 percent of its net income earned over the most recent four-quarter period.

- If the Tier 2 savings association fails to meet its January 1, 1993, capital requirements but does satisfy its January 1, 1991, capital requirements, then it may distribute up to 50 percent of its net income earned over the most recent four-quarter period, without approval.

- Additionally, OTS may approve distributions in excess of the above provisions so long as such actions would be consistent with safe and sound operation of the savings association.

OTS Tier 3 Dividends

Tier 3 savings associations face the sharpest restrictions on dividend distribution.

- OTS must approve all dividend distributions for Tier 3 savings associations. OTS will approve a distribution only when consistent with safe and sound operation of the savings association.

- If the savings association is operating in compliance with an approved capital plan, then the approved distribution must be consistent with the plan. Requests for approval under the capital plan may be made in a combined filing but must be separately identified.

OTS Supervision Restrictions

If OTS has notified a Tier 1 savings association that it is in need of more than normal supervision, it is treated as a Tier 2 or Tier 3 savings association for the purpose of dividend approval unless the OTS determines that such treatment is not necessary.

The OTS District Director has discretion to determine whether to treat such an association as a Tier 2 or Tier 3, and if treated as a Tier 2, to establish which subset of the Tier 2 standards will be applicable.

Future OTS Revision

In January 1998, OTS proposed to simplify its dividend rules. The new rule, if adopted, would change the criteria governing when a savings association must notify or apply to the OTS before paying a dividend. Comments were due in March 1998, suggesting that a final regulation might be issued during the summer of 1998.

References

Laws:

12 U.S.C. 56
12 U.S.C. 60
12 U.S.C. 1467a(f)

Regulations:

12 CFR 5.60-.67 (OCC)
12 CFR 208.19 (FRB)
12 CFR 563.134
12 CFR 567

XII. Environmental Assessments, Compliance, and Lender Liability

Introduction and Purpose 88

Environmental Hazards 88

Environmental Liability 89

General Secured Creditor Exemption 90

Limitations on Fiduciary Liabilities 92

Secured Creditor Exemption for Underground Storage Tanks 93

Environmental Risk Program 95

References 97

Introduction and Purpose

Financial institutions are increasingly exposed to credit risk and liability associated with the cleanup of hazardous substance contamination. The Comprehensive Environmental Response, Compensation and Liability Act (CERCLA), the federal "superfund" statute, and other federal and state statutes establish rules that could require an institution to pay for cleanup costs on real property that the institution holds as collateral.

Congress enacted CERCLA in response to the growing problem of improper handling and disposal of hazardous substances. It authorized the Environmental Protection Agency (EPA) to clean up hazardous waste sites and to recover associated costs from entities specified in the statute.

While CERCLA is the primary federal law dealing with hazardous substance contamination, numerous other federal statutes, as well as state laws, establish environmental liability that could place institutions at risk. For example, underground storage tanks are also covered by separate federal legislation: the Resource Conservation and Recovery Act of 1986.

To limit liability, institutions should have appropriate safeguards and controls in place.

Environmental Hazards

Hazardous substance contamination is most often associated with industrial or manufacturing processes that involve chemicals or solvents in the manufacturing process or as waste products. Hazardous substances are also found in many other lines of business. The following examples demonstrate the diverse sources of potential hazardous substance contamination which should be of concern to financial institutions:

- Farmers and ranchers (use of fuel, fertilizers, herbicides, insecticides, and feedlot runoff);

- Dry cleaners (various cleaning solvents);

- Service station and convenience store operators (underground storage tanks);

- Fertilizer and chemical dealers and applicators (storage and transportation of chemicals);

- Lawn care businesses (application of lawn chemicals); and

- Trucking firms (local and long haul transporters of hazardous substances, such as fuel or chemicals).

An institution should be aware of these and other environmental risks and of the potential liability associated with its activities.

Environmental Liability

CERCLA imposes strict liability on "owners and operators" of facilities contaminated by or containing hazardous substances, and also on those arranging for treatment and disposal of hazardous materials. CERCLA also provides a secured creditor exemption from liability for certain institutions that do not participate in the management of the property. This exemption is discussed further below.

An institution may encounter losses arising from environmental liability in several ways. Of greatest concern are situations where an institution may be held directly liable for cleaning up hazardous-substance contamination. Potential losses also exist where an institution elects to abandon its rights to contaminated real-property collateral because cleanup costs exceed balances owed by borrowers. Additionally, where the credit quality of an individual borrower deteriorates because of the borrower's environmental cleanup responsibility, the borrower's ability to repay a loan may be significantly impaired.

An institution may be held liable for the cleanup of hazardous-substance contamination in situations where the institution:

- Takes title to property under foreclosure;

- Is involved in day-to-day management of the facility through its own personnel or through a contractor;

- Takes actions designed to make the contaminated property salable, possibly resulting in further contamination;

- Acts in a fiduciary capacity, including management involvement in the day-to-day operations of industrial or commercial concerns, and purchasing or selling contaminated property;

- Owns or acquires subsidiaries involved in activities that might result in a finding of environmental liability; or

- Owns or acquires premises that have been previously contaminated by hazardous substances.

General Secured Creditor Exemption

Under CERCLA's secured creditor exemption, an "owner" does not include an institution that, without participating in management, holds the property primarily to protect a security interest. However, some courts have interpreted certain lender actions to be those of "owners and operators" and have allowed EPA to collect cleanup costs from those financial institutions.

The EPA and the Administration have announced that, as a matter of policy, lenders will not be liable for contamination of a borrower's property under certain circumstances. The EPA has also issued a rule clarifying the secured creditor exemption for lenders holding a security interest in underground storage tanks (USTs). (Discussion of this exemption follows the text on the general secured creditor exemption.) However, neither the policy nor the rule is binding on third parties seeking contribution or recovery of costs from an institution.

Congress in 1996 clarified the scope of permissible pre- and postforeclosure activities.

Preforeclosure Activities

Under the new law, a secured creditor participates in management only when the creditor actually participates in the management or operational affairs of a vessel or facility. Participation in management does not include having the capacity to influence, or the unexercised right to control, a vessel or facility.

A lender that holds an indicia of ownership primarily to protect a security interest participates in management preforeclosure only if it:

- Exercises decision-making control over the borrower's environmental compliance, so that the institution has undertaken responsibility for the borrower's hazardous-substance handling or disposal practices; or

- Exercises control at a level comparable to that of a manager, such that the lender has assumed or manifested responsibility for overall management of the vessel or facility (including day-to-day decision making with respect to environmental compliance), or has assumed or manifested responsibility over all or substantially all operational (as opposed to financial or administrative) functions other than environmental compliance.

Activities that do **not** constitute participation in management include:

- Holding, abandoning, or releasing a security interest;

- Including in the terms of an extension of credit, or in a contract or security agreement relating to the extension, a covenant, warranty, or other term or condition that relates to environmental compliance;

- Monitoring or enforcing the terms and conditions of the extension of credit or security interest;

- Monitoring or undertaking one or more inspections of the vessel or facility;

- Requiring a response action or other lawful means of addressing the release or threatened release of a hazardous substance in connection with the vessel or facility prior to, during, or on the expiration of the term of the extension of credit;

- Providing financial or other advice or counseling in an effort to mitigate, prevent, or cure default or diminution in the value of the vessel or facility;

- Restructuring, renegotiating, or otherwise agreeing to alter the terms and conditions of the extension of credit or security interest, exercising forbearance;

- Exercising other remedies that may be available under applicable law for the breach of a term or condition of the extension of credit or security agreement; or

- Conducting a response action.

Postforeclosure Activities

The new law limits the liability of lenders who foreclose on property to protect their security interests. Under the new law, a lender is not an owner or operator if the lender:

- Did not participate in management prior to foreclosure; and

- After foreclosure, seeks to sell, re-lease (in the case of a lease finance transaction), or otherwise divest itself of the vessel or facility at the earliest practicable, commercially reasonable time on commercially reasonable terms.

This limitation on liability applies even if the lender:

- Sells, re-leases (in the case of a lease finance transaction), or liquidates the vessel or facility;

- Maintains business activities;

- Winds up operations;

- Undertakes a response action with respect to the vessel or facility; or

- Takes any other measure to preserve, protect, or prepare the vessel or facility prior to sale or disposition.

An institution must ensure that its activities and the activities of its agents do not worsen any contamination problems. An institution may lose the protection of the secured creditor exemption if the institution improperly handles hazardous substances on the property.

Limitations on Fiduciary Liabilities

The liability of a fiduciary under any provision of CERCLA for any release or threatened release of a hazardous substance cannot exceed the amount of assets held in a fiduciary capacity. A fiduciary will not be personally liable for:

- Undertaking or directing another person to undertake a response action;

- Undertaking or directing another to undertake any other lawful means of addressing a hazardous substance in connection with the vessel or facility;

- Terminating the fiduciary relationship;

- Including in the terms of the fiduciary agreement a covenant, warranty, or other term or condition that relates to compliance with an environmental law, or monitoring, modifying, or enforcing the term or condition;

- Monitoring or undertaking one or more inspections of the facility;

- Providing financial or other advice or counseling to other parties to the fiduciary relationship, including the settlor or beneficiary;

- Restructuring, renegotiating, or otherwise the terms and conditions of the fiduciary relationship; or

- Administering, as a fiduciary, a vessel or facility that was contaminated before the fiduciary relationship began.

This immunity from liability does not extend to:

- A fiduciary whose negligence causes or contributes to the release or threatened release of hazardous substances; or

- A nonemployee agent or independent contractor retained by the fiduciary.

Secured Creditor Exemption for Underground Storage Tanks

The underground storage tank (UST) exemption, which became effective December 6, 1995, limits the regulatory obligations of lenders that:

- Hold a security interest in a UST or tank system or in real estate containing a UST; or

- Acquire title to a UST or property on which a UST is located.

The rule also highlights activities in which lenders may engage during all stages of the secured creditor relationship, from pre-lending through foreclosure and resale.

Within the context of the rule, **underground storage tank** includes any petroleum tank where 10 percent or more of the volume is below the ground's surface. Tanks storing heating oil for consumption on the property and tanks in an underground area but above the floor surface (e.g., tanks in a basement) are not considered USTs.

The exemption outlines the activities that secured creditors may engage in without triggering monitoring, containment, and cleanup responsibilities which fall upon "owners and operators" of USTs.

"Owners and operators" of USTs containing petroleum must:

- Monitor for and report suspected leaks and spills;

- Maintain, inspect, and test corrosion protection;

- Pay cleanup costs for facilities contaminated by leaks or spills;

- Compensate third parties for damages resulting from leaks or spills; and

- Meet financial responsibility requirements.

A lender whose activities are consistent with "holding an indicia of ownership primarily to protect a security interest" does not become an "owner" unless the lender:

- Participates in the management of the UST; or

- Engages in petroleum production, refining, and marketing.

A lender "participates in management" only if the lender exercises decision-making control over and assumes substantially all management of daily operational aspects of the UST. A lender, prior to foreclosure, does not become an "operator" unless the lender is in control of or has responsibility for the daily operation of the UST.

Permissible Pre-Lending Activities

Prior to taking a security interest in the UST or property, no act or omission taken by a lender is considered participating in management. A lender may require a prospective borrower to:

- Conduct an environmental assessment of the UST or property;

- Clean up contamination from the UST; or

- Comply with any applicable law or regulation.

Permissible Loan Oversight and Environmental Compliance Activities

Secured creditors may conduct normal oversight and work-out activities that are consistent with protecting a security interest and do not constitute participation in management. Lenders may also undertake, either during the term of the loan or after foreclosure, certain environmental compliance activities. Permissible oversight and environmental compliance activities include:

- Requiring the borrower to clean up contamination from the UST or to comply with applicable federal, state, and local environmental and other laws, rules, and regulations;

- Detecting and reporting releases from a UST or taking corrective action to reduce or eliminate releases;

- Maintaining a UST's corrosion protection;

- Upgrading and replacing or temporarily or permanently closing a UST;

- Securing or exercising authority to monitor or inspect the UST or property, the borrower's business or financial condition; or

- Taking other oversight actions (such as requiring a borrower to comply with warranties, covenants, or conditions).

The exemption permits the lender to directly oversee these activities and hire contractors to perform the work. However, the lender must conduct these activities according to applicable EPA or state requirements.

Loan Work-Out Activities

A secured creditor may engage in work-out activities prior to foreclosure, provided that it does not participate in the UST's management. The work-out activities include:

- Restructuring or renegotiating the terms of the security interest;

- Requiring payment of additional rent or interest; or

- Exercising any remedy to which the lender is entitled.

Foreclosure

A foreclosing lender remains within the exemption, provided that the lender does not participate in management. The lender must follow specified procedures to attempt to sell, re-lease, or otherwise divest itself of the UST or property. A foreclosing lender loses the exemption's protection if the lender rejects a fair written offer for the property or becomes a UST "operator."

Lenders can avoid "operator" liability if there is an operator who controls the UST's daily operation and can be held responsible for environmental compliance. If another operator does not exist, the lender must, within 60 calendar days of foreclosure, take specified actions to empty and close the UST, or it will be subject to strict liability as an operator.

Environmental Risk Program

To limit the risk of environmental liability, institutions should have an environmental risk program in place. An effective risk program should establish procedures for identifying and evaluating potential environmental concerns associated with lending and nonlending activities (including fiduciary activities) relating to property or equipment. An institution's board of directors should review and approve the program and designate a senior officer knowledgeable in environmental matters to be responsible for program implementation.

The environmental risk program should contain the following:

- **Training.** Staff should be trained to ensure that the risk program is implemented and followed within the institution. Policies should ensure that appropriate personnel have the knowledge and experience to evaluate potential environmental concerns that might affect the institution. Whenever the complexity of an environmental question is beyond the expertise of the institution's staff, the institution should consult legal counsel, environmental consultants, and other qualified experts.

- **Policies.** When appropriate, loan policies, manuals, and written procedures should address environmental matters affecting the institution's specific lending activities. For example, the lending manual might identify the types of environmental risks associated with industries and real estate in the institution's trade area, provide guidelines for conducting an analysis of the potential environmental liability, and describe procedures for the resolution of potential environmental concerns. Institutions may also develop procedures covering credit monitoring, loan work-out situations, and foreclosures.

- **Environmental Risk Analysis.** An institution should conduct an initial environmental risk analysis during the loan application process. Institutions should consider different types of analyses as the risk of environmental liability increases:

    Environmental Review: Screening of the borrower's activities by lending personnel or real estate appraisers for potential environmental problems (using questionnaires, interviews, or observations).

    Environmental Assessment: Structured analysis by a qualified individual that identifies the borrower's past practices, regulatory compliance, and potential future problems. Analysis would include reviewing relevant documents, visiting and inspecting the site, and, in some cases, performing limited tests.

    Environmental Audit: A professional environmental engineer performs a structured analysis similar to an environmental assessment; however, more comprehensive testing might involve collecting and analyzing air samples, and surface and subsurface soil samples, or drilling wells to sample ground water.

- **Loan Documentation.** Loan documents should include language to safeguard the institution against potential environmental losses and liabilities. The institution might require that the borrower comply with environmental laws, disclose information about the environmental status of the real property collateral, and grant the institution the right to acquire additional information about potential hazardous contamination by inspecting the collateral for environmental concerns. Loan documents might also provide that the institution has the right to call the loan, refuse to extend funds under a line of credit, or foreclose if hazardous contamination is discovered in real property collateral.

- **Monitoring.** An institution should assess environmental risk during the life of a loan by monitoring the borrower and real property collateral for potential environmental concerns. The institution should be aware of changes in the business activities of the borrower that result in a significant increased risk of environmental liability associated with the real property collateral.

References

42 U.S.C. 9601 et seq.
40 C.F.R. 280, 281
40 C.F.R. 300 et seq.
FDIC's Guidelines for an Environmental Risk Program
FRB's Environmental Liability Policy

XIII. Foreign Asset Controls

Introduction and Purpose 100

Countries Subject to Asset Control Programs 100

General Scope of Controls 100

Specially Designated Persons and Entities 101

Registration of Blocked Assets 101

Reporting of Transfers 102

Penalties 102

References 102

Introduction and Purpose

The Office of Foreign Assets Control (OFAC) of the U.S. Department of the Treasury administers a series of laws imposing economic sanctions against selected foreign countries. The sanctions implement U.S. foreign policy and national security objectives. OFAC may issue general and specific licenses to authorize transactions otherwise prohibited. The federal financial regulatory agencies are responsible for assuring that financial institutions adhere to these laws.

Countries Subject to Asset Control Programs

The following countries are currently subject to asset control programs under OFAC regulations. Programs change periodically and, occasionally, a country will be added or deleted from the control list.

- Cuba (31 CFR 515)
- Iran (31 CFR 535 and Executive Order 12957)
- Iraq (31 CFR 575)
- Libya (31 CFR 550)
- North Korea (31 CFR 500)
- Unita (Angola) (31 CFR 590)
- Serbia, Montenegro, Bosnia, and Herzegovina (formerly Yugoslavia) (31 CFR 585)

General Scope of Controls

With certain variations, the foreign asset control program in effect for each country covers the following subjects:

- Blocking assets owned or controlled by the foreign government, including government-controlled banks and other corporations.
- Blocking assets owned or controlled by certain individuals in the foreign government or controlling it.
- Blocking imports or exports of goods or services to the foreign country.

- Blocking transportation to or from the foreign country.

- Blocking funds transfers of all kinds to or from entities in the foreign country.

- Blocking credit transactions, including credit cards and credit card processing, involving parties in the foreign country.

- Blocking or tightly controlling payments to individuals in the foreign country.

- Blocking or tightly controlling communications, or payments for communication services, between the U.S. and the foreign country.

- Licensing special exceptions to the assets control program.

Specially Designated Persons and Entities

OFAC publishes a list of "Specially Designated Nationals and Blocked Entities" to alert institutions of status changes. Specially Designated Nationals (SDNs) are individuals or companies which OFAC has designated to be subject to sanctions as if they were a sanctioned government.

In January 1995, OFAC issued a list of "Specially Designated Terrorists" (SDTs) to block persons whom the President designated as terrorist organizations threatening the Middle East peace process. Persons owned or controlled by, or acting for or on behalf of, these terrorist organizations were also included on the list.

In March 1996, OFAC added international narcotics traffickers to its list of Specially Designated Nationals and Blocked Persons.

All transactions and deals are prohibited with any blocked person or entity named in either of these lists.

Registration of Blocked Assets

Institutions holding property subject to foreign sanctions must register the name, title, address, and telephone number of the individual designated to be responsible for the administration of blocked assets, from whom OFAC can obtain information and records. The registration should sent to the Blocked Assets Division, Office of Foreign Assets Control, U.S. Treasury Department, 1500 Pennsylvania Ave., NW C Annex, Washington, DC 20220, within 10 days after the date the institution receives the property. Registrations must be renewed annually on or before July 1.

Reporting of Transfers

Financial institutions receiving instructions to execute payments or transfers into a blocked account must provide written notification to OFAC within 10 business days from the value date of the payment or transfer.

The notification should include a photocopy of the payment or transfer instructions received, and should confirm that the payment or transfer has been deposited into a new or existing blocked account established in the name of the designated national. It should also provide the account number, the name of the account, the location of the account, the name and address of the transferee banking institution, the date of the deposit, the amount of the payment transfer, and the name and telephone number of a contact person at the transferee financial institution from whom compliance information may be obtained. Lastly, the notification should include the name and telephone number of the person who is registered with OFAC and responsible for the administration of blocked assets at the transferee financial institution from whom records on blocked assets may be obtained.

Penalties

A civil penalty fine or imprisonment may be imposed on any person found to be violating economic sanctions regulations. Customs laws also may be applicable to violations of economic sanctions.

Further information on specific economic sanctions may be obtained from the Office of Foreign Assets Control of the U.S. Treasury Department at (202) 622-2500 or from the OFAC information line at (202) 622-2520. Sanctions laws can change rapidly and the OFAC or the Office of Regulatory Affairs should be consulted when an examination raises concerns about compliance with these laws.

References

Laws:

    18 U.S.C. 1001 et seq.
    22 U.S.C. 287c
    22 U.S.C. 2349 et seq.
    50 U.S.C. App. 1-44
    50 U.S.C. 1701 et seq.
    104 Stat. 2047 et seq.
    Executive Order 12947
    Executive Order 12978

Regulations:

    31 C.F.R. Part 595 (OFAC)

XIV. Interbank Liabilities

Introduction and Purpose	104
Prudential Standards	104
Policies and Procedures	104
Correspondent Evaluation	104
Selection of Correspondents by Third Parties	105
Exposure Limits and Monitoring	105
Intraday Exposures	105
Limits on Certain Correspondents	105
Correspondent Capital	105
References	107

Introduction and Purpose

Federal Reserve Board Regulation F requires each insured bank or savings association to control credit risk arising from transactions with other depository institutions, referred to as "correspondents." These controls are implemented through mandatory "prudential standards" for selecting correspondents and monitoring exposure.

Regulation F governs all exposures to correspondent banks, including, but not limited to:

- Correspondent balances;
- Federal funds sold; and
- Loans.

Regulation F became fully effective in June 1995.

Prudential Standards

Policies and Procedures

Each institution's board of directors must adopt and review annually written "prudential" policies and procedures to prevent excessive exposure to any individual correspondent. These policies should establish criteria for selecting correspondents, and for considering credit, liquidity, and operational risks. Regulation F does not require the institution's directors to approve individual correspondent relationships.

Correspondent Evaluation

When a bank's exposure to a correspondent is significant, policies and procedures should require the institution periodically to review the correspondent's financial condition. This review should include analysis of the correspondent's:

- Capital;
- Nonaccrual and past due loans and leases;
- Level of earnings; and
- Other factors affecting the correspondent's financial condition.

A bank may base its review on publicly available information such as call reports and annual reports. While a bank is not required to obtain nonpublic information from its correspondents, it may not ignore nonpublic information to which they have access. A bank may rely on evaluations by third parties. Such third parties include bank holding companies, bank rating agencies, and other correspondents. As a prerequisite to such reliance, however, the bank must review the assessment criteria used by the third party.

Selection of Correspondents by Third Parties

In certain circumstances, an institution may rely on a third party to select its correspondents. For example, a bank may rely on its holding company to select and monitor correspondent relationships. As above, the board of directors must approve and review the selection criteria used by these third parties.

Exposure Limits and Monitoring

When the financial condition of a correspondent creates a "significant risk" that payments will not be made in a timely manner, Regulation F requires institutions to establish correspondent-specific exposure limits. These limits may be fixed, or may be flexible and based on factors such as the level and frequency of exposure monitoring and the condition of the correspondent. These limits are in addition to those discussed below, which are based on the bank's and correspondent's capital.

These limits may be enforced either by monitoring of exposure, or by structuring transactions with correspondents to assure that exposures remain within the institution's internal limits. When monitoring is used, the appropriate level and frequency of monitoring will depend on the type and volatility of the exposure, on the extent to which the exposure approaches the bank's internal limits, and on the condition of the correspondent.

Intraday Exposures

Policies also must address intraday exposures. Policies need only establish specific exposure limits if the size of such exposure and the condition of the correspondent indicate that there is a significant risk that payments will not be made as contemplated.

Limits on Certain Correspondents

Correspondent Capital

In addition to the internal "significant risk" exposure limits discussed above, each institution must limit to 25 percent of its total capital the institution's credit exposure to any correspondent that is less than "adequately capitalized." No limits are specified for adequately or well-capitalized correspondents.

Correspondent Capital Calculation

An adequately capitalized correspondent has:

- A risk-based capital ratio of 8 percent or greater;

- A Tier I risk-based capital ratio of 4 percent or greater; and

- A leverage ratio of 4 percent or greater.

When a correspondent becomes less than adequately capitalized, an institution has 120 days to bring exposure levels into compliance with the limits.

Calculation of correspondent capital adequacy must occur on a timely basis. For domestic banks this calculation must occur quarterly, either from the correspondent's most recent Call Report, financial statement, or bank rating report.

Credit Exposure Calculation

An institution's credit exposure to a correspondent includes its assets and off-balance sheet items that are subject to capital requirements, and that involve claims on a correspondent or capital instruments issued by the correspondent. Off-balance sheet items are valued at their current exposure.

An institution's credit exposure does *not* include:

- Exposure related to settlement of transactions;

- Intraday exposure;

- Transactions in an agency or similar capacity where losses will be passed back to the principal; or

- Other sources of exposure that are not covered in agency capital adequacy guidelines.

In addition, Regulation F allows institutions to exclude the following from the calculation of credit exposure to a correspondent:

- Transactions including reverse repurchase agreements, to the extent that they are secured by government securities or are readily marketable collateral;

- The proceeds of checks and other cash items deposited in an account at a correspondent that are not yet available for withdrawal;

- Certain "quality assets," on which the correspondent is secondarily liable, or on which a creditworthy obligor in addition to the correspondent is available. Regulation F defines quality assets as assets that do not have nonaccrual status:

    a. With principal and interest no more than 30 days past due;

    b. Whose terms have not been renegotiated or compromised due to deteriorating financial conditions of the additional obligor; and

    c. Not classified as "substandard," "doubtful," or "loss" or treated as "other loans specially mentioned" in the most recent report of examination;

- Exposure that results from a merger or acquisition within the last year; and

- The portion of the institution's exposure to the correspondent that is covered by federal deposit insurance.

Waivers

The Federal Reserve Board may grant a waiver of the capital exposure limits in consultation with a bank's primary federal regulator. Banks may be eligible for such a waiver if they are not reasonably able to obtain necessary correspondent services without incurring exposure that exceeds Regulation F's exposure limits.

References

Laws:

    12 U.S.C. 371b-2

Regulations:

    12 CFR Part 206 (Reg. F) (FRB)

XV. International Banking Operations

Introduction and Purpose 110

Foreign Branches of U.S. Banking Institutions 110

Edge and Agreement Corporations 112

Prudential Restrictions on Edge Corporations 115

Investments and Activities Abroad 116

Supervision and Reporting 121

Allocated Transfer Risk Reserve 121

Reporting and Disclosure of International Assets 122

Accounting for Fees on International Loans 122

International Banking Facilities 123

References 124

Commercial Banking Regulatory Handbook

Introduction and Purpose

> Expect changes soon in the Federal Reserve's Regulation K. The comment period for the proposed amendments closed in March 1998. Federal Reserve officials expect to have a final rule in effect by December 31, 1998. We summarize below *in italics* the Federal Reserve's proposed changes.

The Federal Reserve Board's ("Board") Regulation K governs the international and foreign activities of U.S. banking organizations, including:

- National and state member banks;
- Bank holding companies; and
- Edge and Agreement corporations.

The regulation covers the procedures for establishing a foreign branch or Edge or Agreement corporation. It also governs U.S. banking organizations wishing to invest in foreign institutions. FDIC regulations govern the foreign operations of state nonmember banks.

On December 18, 1997, the Federal Reserve Board ("Board") proposed comprehensive revisions to Regulation K. These proposed revisions will be summarized *in italics* at relevant sections of the following discussion. Comments on these proposals are due in March 1998. The Board expects to act on them before year-end 1998.

Foreign Branches of U.S. Banking Institutions

Establishment of Foreign Branches

A foreign branch may be established by:

- A national or state member bank ("member bank");
- An Edge or Agreement corporation; or
- A foreign subsidiary acquired as provided in Regulation K.

The Board proposes to clarify that a member bank may establish foreign branches through an operating subsidiary, with the Board's approval, but only if the foreign branches of the operating subsidiary limit their activities to those permissible for the member bank parent.

A member bank or an Edge or Agreement corporation must obtain the Board's prior approval before establishing its initial branch in any country. A foreign bank subsidiary must obtain the Board's prior approval before establishing its initial branch in its first two countries outside its home country. *The Board proposes to permit any of these banking institutions to establish an initial foreign branch after giving thirty (30) days prior notice to the Board.*

No prior Board approval is required for a banking institution to establish additional branches in any foreign country where it already operates foreign branches. However, a banking organization must give the Board prior notice before establishing a branch in a foreign country even though an affiliated banking entity already operates a branch in that country. *The Board proposes to permit a member bank, an Edge or Agreement corporation, or a foreign bank subsidiary without prior notice to establish an initial branch in any country in which one of its banking affiliates already has a branch. After-the-fact notice would still be required.*

Currently, 45 days prior notice to the Board is required in order for a banking institution (that already has branches in two foreign countries) to branch into additional countries where there is no affiliated banking presence. *The Board has proposed reducing this prior notice to 12 business days.*

Nonbanking subsidiaries held under Regulation K may branch into any country in which any affiliate has a branch after giving 45 days prior notice to the Board. *The Board proposes to permit nonbanking subsidiaries to establish foreign branches without prior review by the Board, subject only to an after-the-fact notice.*

Authority to establish a branch through prior Board approval or notice expires unless the branch actually is established within one year.

Powers of Foreign Branches

A foreign branch of a member bank may engage in the banking activities permitted to the bank under U.S. banking law and its U.S. banking charter. A foreign branch also may engage in the following activities, if doing so is customary for banks in the foreign country:

- Guaranteeing debts or otherwise agreeing to make payments on the occurrence of readily ascertainable events, subject to certain requirements and prudential restrictions.

- Underwriting, distributing, buying, selling, and holding obligations of the foreign government of the country where the branch is located. *The Board proposes to permit branches to underwrite and deal in obligations of governments other than the host government where the branch is located, provided that the obligations are of investment grade.*

- Investing in securities of the central bank, local clearinghouses, and development banks of the country where the branch is located, if these investments do not exceed 1 percent of the branch's total deposits as reported on the preceding year-end call report date.

- Making loans to local officers to finance the acquisition of living quarters abroad, subject to certain reporting requirements. *The Board proposes to amend the requirements to make them consistent with the more liberalized Regulation O.*

- Making real estate loans, whether or not of first priority and whether or not the real estate has been improved.

- Acting as insurance agent or broker.

- Paying greater rates of interest on deposits to employees as part of a benefits program.

- Engaging in repurchase agreements involving securities and commodities that are the functional equivalent of extensions of credit.

- Investing in subsidiaries (with Board approval) that engage solely in permissible U.S. banking activities or activities which are incidental to the branch's business.

- Undertaking (with Board approval) other activities usual in connection with the business of banking in the foreign country.

Edge and Agreement Corporations

U.S. banking institutions, with prior Board approval, may establish Edge corporations and Agreement corporations to conduct international banking, financial, and investment activities. Edge and Agreement corporations must meet a variety of regulatory standards and requirements to assure their international character.

Edge Corporations

Board Approval

The Board itself charters Edge corporations. When reviewing a U.S. banking institution's proposal to establish an Edge corporation, the Board considers the following factors:

International Banking Operations 113

- The financial condition and history of the applicant;

- The general character of its management;

- The convenience and needs of the community to be served (with respect to international banking and financing services); and

- The effects of the proposal on competition.

Upon approval, the Board issues a permit that allows the Edge corporation to commence business.

Change of Control

Any person must give the Board 60 days written notice before acquiring (directly or indirectly) 25 percent or more of the voting shares or otherwise taking control of an Edge corporation. The Board may extend the 60-day period by an additional 30 days. After considering the relevant factors (see the Board Approval factors above), the Board may disapprove the acquisition or impose regulatory conditions on the acquisition.

Domestic Branches

An Edge corporation may establish a branch anywhere in the United States, 45 days after providing its Federal Reserve Bank with proper notice. This notice must include a copy of the Edge corporation's proposal published in a newspaper that serves the same community as the potential branch. The proposal must appear in the newspaper within 90 days preceding notice to the Reserve Bank, and advise the public that it has 30 days to comment on the proposal.

In acting upon a branch proposal, the Board considers the same factors as in approving a charter.

Permissible Activities in the United States

An Edge corporation may engage directly or indirectly in activities in the United States that are permitted by Section 25(a) of the Federal Reserve Act and which are incidental to international or foreign business. Such activities include:

- **Deposit activities.** An Edge corporation may receive in the United States transaction accounts, savings, and time deposits (including issuing negotiable certificates of deposit) from foreign governments (including their agencies and instrumentalities) and foreign persons, as well as from other persons in specified situations related to international transactions.

- **Liquid funds.** An Edge corporation may invest or hold funds that are not currently used in its international business in the form of certain liquid U.S. investments (e.g., as cash, money market instruments, U.S. government obligations, and deposits with depository institutions and other Edge or Agreement corporations).

- **Borrowing.** An Edge corporation may borrow from other Edge and Agreement corporations, foreign banks and depository institutions, incur indebtedness in connection with repurchase transactions, and issue long-term subordinated debt.

- **Credit activities.** An Edge corporation may finance imports and exports and foreign contracts, projects or activities abroad, the production of goods for export, the domestic shipment of exports and imports, and other international transactions. It may also guarantee debts and provide credit and other banking services involving international transactions.

- **Payments and collections.** An Edge corporation may receive checks, bills, notes, bonds, and other instruments for collection abroad, perform collection activities, and handle certain wire transfers.

- **Foreign exchange.** An Edge corporation may engage in foreign exchange activities.

- **Fiduciary and investment advisory activities.** An Edge corporation may engage in international fiduciary and investment advisory activities.

- **Banking services for employees.** An Edge corporation may provide certain banking services (including deposit services) to its officers and employees (and those of its affiliates), subject to U.S. insider lending restrictions.

Agreement Corporations

Subject to Board approval, U.S. banking institutions may also invest in an Agreement corporation. An Agreement corporation is a state-chartered international banking corporation that enters into an agreement with the Board to limit its activities to those permitted to an Edge corporation.

International Banking Operations

Prudential Restrictions on Edge Corporations

Acceptances of Edge Corporations

An Edge corporation must be and remain fully secured for:

- All acceptances outstanding in excess of 200 percent of its Tier I capital; and

- All acceptances outstanding for any one person in excess of 10 percent of its Tier I capital.

Exceptions

The above limitations do not apply if the excess represents the international shipment of goods and the Edge corporation is:

- Fully covered by primary obligations to reimburse it that are guaranteed by banks or bankers; or

- Covered by qualifying agreements from other banks.

Lending Limits

An Edge corporation engaged in banking — defined as an Edge corporation which is ordinarily engaged in the business of accepting deposits in the United States from nonaffiliated persons — and its subsidiaries may not have total loans and extensions of credit outstanding to any person in excess of 15 percent of its Tier I capital. In addition, the total loans and extensions of credit to any person by a foreign bank or Edge corporation subsidiary (of a member bank), and by majority-owned subsidiaries of a foreign bank or Edge corporation, when combined with the total loans and extensions of credit to the same person by the member bank (and its majority-owned subsidiaries), may not exceed the member bank's limit on loans and extensions of credit to one person.

Loans and extensions of credit covered by the above lending limits are defined as all direct and indirect advances of funds to a person made on the basis of any obligation of that person to repay funds, and specifically includes:

- Certain acceptances outstanding;

- Any liability of the lender to advance funds to, or on behalf of, a person pursuant to a guarantee, standby letter of credit, or similar agreement;

- Investments in the securities of another institution (not a subsidiary); and

- Any underwriting commitment to an issuer of securities where no binding commitments have been secured from sub-underwriters or other purchasers.

Exceptions

The above lending limits do not apply to:

- Deposits with banks and federal funds sold;

- Bills or drafts drawn in good faith against goods, on which two or more unrelated parties are liable;

- Any eligible banker's acceptance that is issued and outstanding;

- Obligations to the extent secured by cash or bonds, notes, certificates of indebtedness or T-bills of the United States;

- Loans and extensions of credit that are covered by *bona fide* participation agreements; and

- Obligations to the extent supported by the full faith and credit of the United States, its agencies or departments, international developmental banks, or other related organizations.

Capitalization

An Edge corporation must remain adequately capitalized at all times. An Edge corporation engaged in banking should have a minimum ratio of qualifying total capital to risk-weighted assets, as determined under the Capital Adequacy Guidelines, of not less than 10 percent, of which at least 50 percent should consist of Tier 1 capital; provided that for purposes of such calculations, no limitation shall apply on the inclusion of subordinated debt that qualifies as Tier 2 capital under the Capital Adequacy Guidelines.

Investments and Activities Abroad

Member banks, bank holding companies, and Edge or Agreement corporations may make certain investments outside the United States. These "investors" may make:

- A foreign **portfolio** investment in an organization in which the investor (and its affiliates) holds less than 20 percent of the voting shares and does not otherwise control the organization;

- A foreign **joint venture** investment in an organization in which the investor (and its affiliates) holds 20 percent but not more than 50 percent of the voting shares of an organization, and which it does not otherwise control; or

- A **foreign subsidiary** investment in an organization in which an investor (and its affiliates) holds more than 50 percent of the voting shares or total equity of the organization or otherwise exercises control.

A member bank, however, may make direct investments only in foreign banks or in corporations performing nominee, fiduciary, or other permissible incidental banking activities abroad.

*The Board proposes to increase the limit on **portfolio investments** to less than 25 percent of a company's voting shares. The Board proposes also to revise the definition of a **joint venture investment** to include a company in which an investor (and its affiliates) has 25 percent or more of its voting shares, but which is not a subsidiary of the investor.*

Permissible Activities

Except as noted below, an investor's foreign subsidiary or foreign joint venture may engage only in the following banking or financial activities, which the Board has determined are usual in connection with banking and other financial operations abroad:

- Commercial and other banking activities;

- Financing (including commercial and consumer financing, mortgage banking, and factoring);

- Leasing real or personal property, or acting as agent, broker, or advisor in such leasing (if the lease serves as the functional equivalent of an extension of credit). *The Board proposes to remove this limitation for high residual value leasing as permitted to bank holding companies under Regulation Y*;

- Acting as a fiduciary;

- Underwriting credit life insurance and credit accident and health insurance;

- Performing services for other direct or indirect operations of a U.S. banking institution;

- Holding the premises of overseas branches or subsidiaries;

- Providing investment, financial, or economic advisory services;

- General insurance agency and brokerage;

- Data processing;

- Organizing, sponsoring, and managing a mutual fund (if the funds are not sold or distributed in the U.S. or to U.S. residents and the fund does not control the firms it invests in);

- Performing management consulting services (if for the U.S. market, initial entry only);

- Underwriting, dealing, and distributing debt securities outside of the United States;

- Underwriting, dealing, and distributing equity securities outside of the United States, subject to certain limitations and restrictions, based generally on certain dollar or percentage of capital limits on underwriting and dealing exposure. *The Board proposes to eliminate the dollar limits on foreign underwriting and dealing exposure for banking institutions considered to be well capitalized and well managed. For such institutions, the limits would be based solely on percentages of the institution's Tier 1 capital*;

- Operating a travel agency (if it is in connection with financial services offered abroad);

- Underwriting life, annuity, pension fund-related, and other types of insurance if the risks have been found to be actuarially predictable and subject to certain prudential conditions, including the limitation of such investments to bank holding company investors. *The Board requests comment on whether the reinsuring by a foreign subsidiary of a bank holding company of annuities or life insurance policies sold to U.S. persons is an activity that should be considered to fall within this authority*;

- Acting as a futures commission merchant for financial instruments that the Board has approved subject to the limitations and requirements of Regulation Y for bank holding companies and prior approval for activities conducted on any exchange that requires members to guarantee or otherwise cover losses of other members. *The Board proposes to eliminate the prior approval requirement when the activity is conducted through a separately incorporated subsidiary of the bank and the parent bank does not provide a guarantee or otherwise become liable to an exchange or clearinghouse for an amount in excess of the general consent limits for investments (discussed below);*

- Acting as a principal or agent in a swap transaction, subject to certain limitations. *The Board proposes to harmonize these limitations with those applicable to bank holding companies, so that commodity-related swaps would not require a cash settlement;*

- Engaging in activities that the Board has found to be closely related to banking under its Regulation Y; and

- Engaging in other activities that the Board has determined to be closely related to banking.

Up to 5 percent of a subsidiary's consolidated assets and revenues may be attributed to activities that are not permissible under the foregoing list. Up to 10 percent of a foreign joint venture's consolidated assets and revenues may be so attributed.

While no activity restrictions apply to portfolio investments, Regulation K imposes on investors certain aggregate limits on such portfolio investments tied to a percentage of the investor's capital. *The Board proposes to liberalize these aggregate limits for portfolio investments of bank holding companies that are well capitalized and well managed.*

Investment Procedures

Direct and indirect investment procedures require different forms of Board approval, depending on the type and size of the investment. The three main categories of approval are general consent, prior notice, and specific consent.

General Consent

The Board grants its general consent for the following investments in permissible activities:

- Any investment in a joint venture or subsidiary, and any portfolio investment if the total amount invested does not exceed the lesser of:

    – $25 million; or

    – 5 percent of the investor's Tier I capital (of a member bank, bank holding company, or Edge corporation engaged in banking) or 25 percent of the investor's Tier I capital (if an Edge corporation is not engaged in banking);

- Any additional investment in an organization in any calendar year, if:

  — The total amount invested in that year does not exceed 10 percent of the investor's Tier I capital; and the total amount invested in that calendar year (including under specific-consent and prior-notice procedures) does not exceed cash dividends reinvested plus 10 percent of the investor's historical cost in the organization, which investment authority (to the extent unexercised) may be carried forward and accumulated for five years;

  — Any other investment in an organization in an amount equal to cash dividends received from that organization during the preceding 12 calendar months; or

  — Any investment that is acquired from an affiliate at net asset value.

Prior Notice

If an investor's proposed investment in permissible activities exceeds the amounts approved under the Board's general consent, then the investor should notify the Board 45 days before making the investment. The investment is permitted if the 45 days expires without Board action. The Board may waive the notice period or suspend the period or act on the investment under specific consent procedures.

Specific Consent

An investment that does not qualify for general-consent or prior-notice procedures requires the specific prior consent of the Board.

The Board has proposed that only significant investments, as determined solely on the basis of the investor's capital, would be subject to prior review by the Board, provided that the investors are well-capitalized and well-managed.

Other Investments

- **Debts Previously Contracted.** An investor may acquire stock or other ownership interest to prevent losses on debts previously contracted, if the acquisition is disposed of within two years, or such longer period as the Board permits.

International Banking Operations

- **Debt-for-Equity Swaps.** A bank holding company may convert the sovereign or private debt obligations of an "eligible country" into an equity investment. An "eligible country" is one that has restructured its sovereign debt since 1980. *The Board has proposed that the term "eligible country" be redefined so that only countries with currently impaired sovereign debt would be eligible for investments through debt-for-equity swaps.* An investor bank holding company may acquire through such a swap up to 100 percent of the ownership of a public company, if the shares are acquired from the foreign government. In the case of a private sector company, an investor may acquire no more than 40 percent of the shares, and is subject to other limits on its control of the company. In some situations, the Board may permit a debt-for-equity investment to be made indirectly through a U.S. bank subsidiary of a bank holding company. Debt-for-equity investments must normally be disposed of within 10 years, unless extended by the Board.

Supervision and Reporting

U.S. banking institutions must supervise and administer their foreign branches and subsidiaries to ensure that high standards of banking and financial prudence are met. Effective systems of records, controls, and reports on the condition and activities of a U.S. banking institution's branches and subsidiaries must be maintained to inform management, including reports on risk assets. Reports on operations and controls must include internal and external audits. Specified information and audits must also be maintained on joint venture investments. All required reports and information must be made available to examiners. Edge and Agreement corporations must also file the same criminal referral report forms as member banks. Certain reports, including those on foreign operations and the acquisition or disposition of shares, must be filed with the appropriate Federal Reserve Bank. Edge corporations must also be examined at least once a year.

Allocated Transfer Risk Reserve

Transfer risk means the possibility that an asset cannot be serviced in the currency of payment because of a lack of, or restraints on the availability of, needed foreign exchange in the country of the obligor.

If required by the Board, a U.S. banking institution must establish an allocated transfer risk reserve ("ATRR") for specified international assets. At least annually, the federal banking agencies will jointly determine ATRR requirements and levels.

Accounting Treatment for ATRR

A banking institution must establish an ATRR by a charge to current income. This charge may not be included in capital or surplus. An ATRR must be established on a consolidated basis and accounted for separately from the allowance for possible loan losses. A bank need not establish an ATRR if it writes down (or has written down in prior periods) the value of the specified international assets for which the ATRR is required.

Reporting and Disclosures of International Assets

At least quarterly, each U.S. banking institution must submit to the Board information on the amount and composition of its international assets. Each institution must also report the concentration of its international assets that are material in relation to its total assets and capital. The Board may require additional or more frequent reporting if it is deemed necessary.

Accounting for Fees on International Loans

Restructured International Loans

No U.S. banking institution may charge fees for a restructured international loan unless all fees exceeding the institution's administrative costs are deferred and recognized over the term of the loan as an interest-yield adjustment.

Amortizing Fees

Unless otherwise provided under Regulation K, fees received on international loans must be deferred and amortized over the term of the loan. The interest method should be used during the loan period to recognize the deferred fee revenue in relation to the outstanding balance. If the interest method is impractical, the straight-line method should be used instead.

Administrative Costs

The administrative costs of originating, restructuring, or syndicating an international loan should be expended as incurred. These costs include costs associated with negotiating, processing, and consummating a loan, such as legal fees and processing costs. The portion of the fee income equal to the institution's administrative costs may be recognized as income in the same period that the costs are expended.

Fees Received by Managing Banking Institutions

In general, fees received on international syndicated loans representing an adjustment of the yield on the loan should be recognized over the loan period using the interest rate method. If the interest-yield portion of a fee received on an international syndicated loan by a managing bank is unstated or differs materially from the *pro rata* portion paid other participants, an amount necessary for an interest-yield adjustment must be recognized.

Loan Commitment Fees

Loan commitment fees based on the unfunded portion of a credit for the period until it is drawn should be recognized as income over the term of the commitment period. Commitment fees for revolving-credit arrangements (where fees are received periodically in arrears and are based on the amount of the unused loan commitment) may be recognized as income when received if the income result would not be materially different.

If it is impractical to separate the commitment portion from the other fee components, the entire fee should be amortized over the term of the combined commitment and expected loan period.

Agency Fees

Agency fees are fees paid to an agent banking institution for administrative services in an international syndicated loan. They should be recognized at the time of the loan closing or as the service is performed, whichever is later.

International Banking Facilities

An **international banking facility** ("IBF") is a set of accounts segregated on the books and records of a depository institution in the United States. The IBF may include only IBF time deposits and loans, as well as the income and expense accounts relating to those IBF loans and deposits.

IBF time deposits:

- Must remain on deposit at the IBF at least overnight;

- May only be issued to other offices of the institution establishing the IBF and certain specified foreign persons and institutions;

- May not be payable in less than two business days; and

- May only be used to support the operations outside the United States of the depositor or its affiliates.

IBF loans may only be extended to other offices of the institution establishing the IBF and certain specified foreign persons and institutions. U.S. depository institutions, Edge Act and Agreement corporations, and U.S. branches and agencies of foreign banks may establish IBFs.

An IBF is the banking equivalent of a free trade zone. An institution booking deposits in an IBF may maintain them free of reserve requirements and free from deposit insurance premiums. Thus, the IBF has a lower cost of funds than an insured bank providing identical services. It is intended to provide U.S. banks with competitive funding opportunities in international markets without having to establish an offshore branch.

References

Laws:

12 U.S.C. 461(b)
12 U.S.C. 601-604a
12 U.S.C. 611 et seq.
12 U.S.C. 1843(c)(13)
12 U.S.C. 3901 et seq.

Regulations:

12 CFR 211 (Regulation K)
12 CFR 204 (Regulation D)

XVI. Lease Financing

Introduction and Purpose 126

Leasing Requirements for National Banks 126

General Rule 126

CEBA Leases 127

Full-Payout Leases 127

Leasing Requirements for Federal Savings Associations 128

Finance Leases 128

General Leases 129

Leasing Salvage Powers 129

References 129

Introduction and Purpose

Federal law permits national banks and federally chartered savings associations to lease personal property for consumer and commercial purposes, provided the lease is the functional equivalent of a secured loan. Federally chartered savings associations are permitted also to offer such finance leases for real property. The OCC and OTS have adopted similar regulations governing leasing activities. State law governs the power of state-chartered institutions to lease personal property.

Leasing Requirements for National Banks

National banks are authorized to finance leases under two sections in the National Bank Act.

12 U.S.C. 24 (Seventh) permits national banks to engage in the "business of banking." The OCC and the courts interpret this statute to allow banks to engage in lease financing.

12 U.S.C. 24 (Tenth) specifically authorizes a national bank to invest in personal property to be used in lease financing transactions. It was added by the Competitive Equality Banking Act of 1987 (CEBA) to relieve national banks from the residual value restrictions imposed by the OCC, and to allow shorter-term leases.

An OCC regulation implements both statutes.

General Rule

OCC's regulation requires a national bank to write its leases on terms that reasonably anticipate a return of the bank's full investment in the leased property, plus the estimated cost of financing the property. The sources of repayment include lease payments, estimated tax benefits, and the estimated residual value of the property.

All leases by national banks generally must be on a *net lease basis*. Under a net lease, the bank may not be responsible for repair, maintenance, insurance, licensing, or replacement of the property. All responsibilities of ownership must be transferred to the lessee during the lease.

A national bank may, however, take "reasonable and appropriate" action to salvage or protect the property's worth if the bank believes some unexpected event significantly increases its exposure. A national bank also may engage in various marketing, finder, or other activities, including arranging for services prohibited for banks to be performed by third parties, without compromising its net lease basis status.

Before a national bank may acquire property to be leased, it must have either:

- A legally binding commitment to lease the property; or

- A written indemnification against loss.

When a lease expires, a national bank either must liquidate all of its interest in the property or release the property within five years of the bank acquiring legal right to possession or control of the property. The OCC may extend the holding period for up to an additional five years, if the bank clearly convinces the agency that it needs an additional holding period.

Lease transactions are subject both to the limits on extensions of credit to any one borrower, and to the restrictions on transactions with a bank affiliate. For these purposes, transactions are valued at the bank's investment in the property, net of any nonrecourse financing.

CEBA Leases

A national bank may use its authority under CEBA to acquire and lease only tangible personal property, such as vehicles, manufactured homes, machinery, equipment, or furniture. A CEBA lease may permit the lessee to cancel the lease after an initial 90-day period. When the lease is canceled before it expires, the property returned to the bank may exceed 25 percent of its original value. CEBA thus permits a partial payout lease.

To limit the risk of partial payout leases, a bank's aggregate investment in property leased under CEBA may not exceed 10 percent of its consolidated assets. The aggregate investment is calculated net of any nonrecourse financing for the property.

A national bank may purchase both a lease and the related tangible property from another lessor. The bank may acquire existing leases with maturities of less than 90 days if original lease terms conformed to OCC rules. A bank's records must identify which leases are CEBA leases.

Full-Payout Leases

A national bank may use its general banking authority of 12 U.S.C. 24 (Seventh) to acquire and lease personal property that is either tangible or intangible, such as copyrights or other intellectual property. While all national banks' finance leases must be on a net basis, leases authorized by 12 U.S.C. 24 (Seventh) also must be on a full-payout basis and represent a noncancelable obligation of the lessee.

Under a *full-payout lease*, the unguaranteed portion of the estimated residual value relied upon by the bank to yield a full return cannot exceed 25 percent of the original cost of the property. Thus, a national bank must recover at least 75 percent of the original cost of the property from rentals and estimated tax benefits, plus estimated financing costs. To enter a leasing transaction, a national bank must rely on the creditworthiness of the lessee, not the residual value of the property.

Leasing Requirements for Federal Savings Associations

The OTS regulations distinguish the two types of leasing activities allowed for federally chartered savings associations: "finance leases" and "general leases."

Finance Leases

OTS permits a savings association to conduct its lending activities by acquiring either real or personal property and leasing that property under finance leases that are the functional equivalent of loans. To qualify as a financing lease:

- The lease must be a net, full-payout lease representing a noncancelable obligation of the lessee, notwithstanding the possible early termination of the lease;

- The portion of the estimated residual value of the property relied upon by the lessor to satisfy the requirements of a full-payout lease must be reasonable in light of the nature of the leased property and all relevant circumstances so that realization of the lessor's full investment plus the cost of financing the property depends primarily on the creditworthiness of the lessee, and not on the residual market value of the leased property; and

- At the termination of a financing lease either by expiration or default, property acquired must be liquidated or re-leased on a net basis as soon as practicable. Any property held in anticipation of re-leasing must be reevaluated and recorded at the lower of fair market or book value.

Financing leases are subject to the same investment limits imposed by the Homeowner's Loan Act (HOLA) that apply to residential real estate loans; commercial, business, corporate, or agricultural loans; nonresidential real estate loans; and consumer loans. For example, a financing lease of tangible personal property made to a natural person for personal, family, or household purposes is subject to the limitations that apply to an association's investment in consumer loans.

General Leases

A savings association may invest in tangible personal property, including vehicles, manufactured homes, machinery, equipment, or furniture for the purpose of leasing that property as long as these investments do not exceed 10 percent of the savings association's assets. General leases do not need to be the functional equivalent of loans.

Leasing Salvage Powers

If a savings association believes that an unanticipated change in conditions that significantly increased its exposure to loss occurred, it may in good faith:

- As the owner and lessor, take reasonable and appropriate action to salvage or protect the value of the property or its interest arising under the lease;

- As the assignee of a lessor's interest in a lease, become the owner and lessor of the leased property pursuant to its contractual right, or take any reasonable and appropriate action to salvage or protect the value of the property or its interest arising under the lease; or

- Include any provisions in a lease, or make additional agreements, to protect its financial position or investment in the circumstances set for above.

References

Laws:

   12 U.S.C. 24
   12 U.S.C. 1464

Regulations:

   12 CFR Part 23 (OCC)
   12 CFR 560.41 (OTS)

XVII. Lending Limits

Introduction and Purpose 132

General Limitations 132

Definitions 132

Collateral Procedures 134

Combining Loans to Separate Borrowers 134

Nonconforming Loans 135

Commitments to Advance Funds 136

Exceptions and Exclusions to the Lending Limits 139

Exceptions for Savings Associations 140

References 141

Introduction and Purpose

Every depository institution is subject to restrictions concerning the amount of money that it may lend to a single borrower. This section focuses specifically on the statutory lending limit applicable to national banks set out in 12 U.S.C. 84. A state-chartered bank must comply with the single borrower restrictions of its home state, which often is similar to the limits for national banks. The national bank lending limit also applies, with minor modifications, to both federal- and state-chartered savings associations.

The purpose of statutory lending limits is to diversify risk and to spread credit availability among large numbers of persons. Every bank should have a system to monitor compliance with these limits, including the aggregation, where required, of loans to related borrowers.

General Limitations

Unsecured Loans

A national bank may lend or extend credit unsecured to any one borrower, or group of related borrowers, totaling up to 15 percent of the bank's capital and surplus.

Secured Loans

The 15 percent lending limit is raised to 25 percent of capital and surplus if the incremental 10 percent is secured fully by readily marketable collateral having a market value at least equal to the amount of the loans or extensions of credit.

Definitions

Loans and extensions of credit means any direct or indirect advance of funds to a person:

- Made on the basis of any obligation of that person to repay the funds; or

- Repayable from specific property pledged by or on behalf of a person.

The term includes contractual commitments to advance funds.

Person means an individual, sole proprietorship, partnership, joint venture, association, trust, estate, business trust, corporation, nonprofit organization, sovereign government or agency, instrumentality, or political subdivision thereof, or any similar entity or organization.

Lending Limits 133

Contractual commitment to advance funds means:

- An obligation to make payments to a third party, contingent upon a default by the bank's customer in the performance of a contract with the third party;

- An obligation to guarantee or stand as surety for the benefit of a third party; or

- A qualifying commitment to lend.

Contractual commitments include:

- Standby letters of credit;

- Guarantees;

- Puts;

- Surety obligations; and

- Other similar arrangements.

Capital and surplus includes:

- Tier I and Tier II capital reported in the most recent "Call Report" (see Capital Adequacy);

- The balance of the general allowance for loan and lease losses not included in Tier II capital; and

- For thrifts, investments in subsidiaries not included in Tier I capital.

Generally, capital and surplus is determined quarterly, based on Call Report data. More frequent calculation may be required at the discretion of the regulator for safety and soundness purposes, and when there is a change in the bank or thrift's prompt corrective action category.

Readily marketable collateral includes:

- Stocks, notes, bonds, and debentures traded on a national securities exchange;

- OTC margin stocks;

- Bullion;

- Commercial paper;
- Negotiable certificates of deposit;
- Bankers' acceptances; and
- Shares in money market and mutual funds of the type that issue shares in which a bank may perfect a security interest.

Collateral Procedures

Each bank must institute adequate procedures to ensure that the collateral value fully secures the outstanding loan at all times.

When collateral values fall below 100 percent of the outstanding loan, to the extent that the loan exceeds the general 15 percent limitation, the loan generally must be brought into conformance within 30 business days.

Combining Loans to Separate Borrowers

The most common violation of these limits occurs from the failure to combine, for lending limit purposes, credit extended to different but related borrowers.

Loans and extensions of credit will be attributed to other customers for purposes of lending limit calculations when the proceeds are to be used for the direct benefit of the others, or when there is a "common enterprise."

A **common enterprise** occurs when:

- Expected source of repayment is the same;
- Loans are made to customers who are related through common control, if they are engaged in an interdependent business or if there is a substantial financial interdependence among them; or
- Separate customers borrow to acquire a business enterprise that will be controlled by them (50 percent or more of the voting stock).

Corporations

Loans to a parent corporation and its subsidiaries are not combined unless they are engaged in a common enterprise. However, the total loans and credit extensions to a corporation and all subsidiaries cannot exceed 50 percent of the bank's capital and surplus.

Partnerships

Loans to a customer who is involved as a principal in a partnership, a joint venture, or an association usually are combined with loans to the partnership (joint venture, etc.) for determining the customer's lending limit. Loans to two or more members of a partnership normally are not combined, but may be combined if used to support the partnership or another common enterprise.

Foreign Governments

Loans to foreign government-owned corporations will be combined, for lending limit purposes, if they fail to meet either the following means or purpose tests at the time the loan or extension of credit is made:

- **Means test.** The borrower has resources or revenues of its own sufficient over time to service its debt obligation; or

- **Purpose test.** The purpose of the loan or extension of credit is consistent with purposes of the borrower's general business.

To demonstrate that the means or purpose tests have been satisfied, a bank must assemble and retain in its files these documents:

- A statement describing the legal status and degree of financial and operational autonomy of the borrowing entity;

- Three-year financial statements of the borrowing entity;

- Financial statements for each year the loan or extension of credit is outstanding;

- The bank's assessments of the borrower's means of servicing the loan; and

- The loan agreement or other written statement from the borrower clearly describing the purpose of the loan or extension of credit.

Nonconforming Loans

The OCC's lending limit rule recognizes a "nonconforming" loan category. This category provides relief for certain technical lending limit violations, which otherwise might be deemed violations of law and subject to possible civil money penalties or other regulatory sanction.

Nonconforming loans include loans which were made within the legal lending limits but no longer fall within the current lending limits due to:

- The following circumstances, for which an institution must use reasonable efforts to bring the loan(s) into compliance unless doing so would be inconsistent with safe and sound banking practices:

    – A decline in the lending institution's capital;

    – Subsequent merger of borrowers or formation of a common enterprise;

    – Subsequent merger of lenders; or

    – A change in the regulatory capital rules; or

- A decline in the value of collateral securing a loan which previously satisfied a lending limit exception, and which a lending institution must bring into conformity within 30 calendar days, except in the case of judicial proceedings, regulatory actions, or other extraordinary circumstances beyond the institution's control.

Commitments to Advance Funds

Funding of Commitments

A legally binding written loan commitment qualifies as a loan and can be funded during its entire term, even if the bank's lending limit subsequently declines. However, the commitment, when combined with other loans to the borrower, must have been within the bank's lending limit at the time the commitment was made.

Other types of commitments, including oral commitments and legally binding written loan commitments, will not qualify as loans if combinations with other outstanding loans and qualifying commitments exceed the bank's lending limit on the date of execution. These types of commitments may be funded only if they are within the bank's lending limit on the date of funding.

A qualifying loan commitment can be funded regardless of the bank's lending limit at the time of funding; however, any funded amounts in excess of the bank's lending limit at the time of funding are deemed "nonconforming" for purposes of Section 84. A bank may not advance additional credit to a borrower whose loans with the bank have become nonconforming, except in certain circumstances, as described under exceptions and exclusions on the next page.

Lending Limits   137

Example:

June	Bank's lending limit is $10 million. Bank loans $5 million to Borrower.
July	Bank enters into loan commitment with Borrower for additional $5 million with maturity of one year.
	Because commitment is within lending limit when made, it qualifies as a loan.
October	Bank's lending limit declines to $7 million and Borrower asks that the bank fully fund its July loan commitment.
	Because commitment qualified as a loan when made, the bank can fund the commitment without violating Section 84. The amount in excess of its lending limit, $3 million, would be deemed nonconforming.
November	Borrower requests short-term loan of $500,000.
	Because of outstanding nonconforming loans, the bank could not make this loan without violating Section 84.

Subsequent Loans in Excess of Lending Limits

A bank that has reached its lending limit to a borrower through combination of outstanding loans and unfunded commitments qualifying as loans may continue to extend credit to that borrower. However, if the bank does extend an additional loan to the borrower, the unfunded commitment automatically will be disqualified from being treated as a loan and will be treated as a loan commitment. Subsequent loans operate to disqualify the entire unfunded portions of prior qualifying loan commitments in reverse chronological order. Disqualified commitments need not be included in a bank's lending limit calculation until funds are advanced.

Example:

Throughout the year, Bank's lending limit is $10 million.

June	Bank loans $5 million to Borrower.
July	Bank issues $5 million qualifying loan commitment to Borrower.
August	Borrower requests additional loan of $1 million (unrelated to the qualifying loan commitment, which is still unfunded).

Bank can make the $1 million loan, thereby disqualifying the unfunded loan commitment made in July. The disqualified loan commitment then could be funded only to the extent that the advance (combined with all other outstanding loans and qualifying commitments) does not exceed the lending limit on the day of funding. The bank could advance only $4 million under the commitment.

If Borrower had requested a second loan commitment of $1 million in August, rather than a loan, the July loan commitment would not have been disqualified. A qualifying loan commitment may be disqualified only by a subsequent loan that would cause the bank to exceed its lending limit. A loan commitment of $1 million in August would not have qualified as a loan and therefore would not have disqualified the July loan commitment.

Renewals

Upon the expiration of an unfunded or partially funded loan commitment, the bank must exercise its best efforts to conform that commitment with the bank's current lending limit.

Any renewal of a funded portion of a commitment in excess of the lending limit will be deemed nonconforming rather than a violation.

A renewal of an unfunded commitment in excess of the lending limit will be treated as any loan commitment (i.e., not a violation of Section 84).

Example:

June 1996	Bank's lending limit is $10 million. Bank enters into a $10 million qualifying loan commitment for one year with Borrower.
October 1996	Bank advances $7 million under qualifying commitment to Borrower A.
June 1997	Bank's lending limit decreases to $5 million. Borrower requests that the entire commitment be renewed.

Bank must use its best efforts to bring $7 million into conformance with lending limit of $5 million. If unable to, bank may renew the funded portion for $7 million. Upon renewal, $2 million of funded portion will be deemed nonconforming.

If Borrower requests that the bank renew its commitment as a revolving credit, the bank will be permitted to renew only $5 million, an amount within its lending limit.

The renewal of the unfunded $3 million will not by itself constitute a violation of Section 84. A violation will occur, however, if on the date the bank advances the funds, the amount exceeds the bank's lending limit.

Exceptions and Exclusions to the Lending Limits

Loans and extensions of credit may exceed the general lending limit if they qualify under one of the following exceptions or exclusions:

1. **Discounting of commercial paper.** No limit applies to obligations arising from the discounting of negotiable instruments given in payment of the purchase price of commodities, where the delivery of the commodities may reasonably be expected to provide funds for payment of the paper. The paper must bear the full recourse endorsement of the owner.

2. **Bankers' acceptances.** The bank may purchase eligible bankers' acceptances without regard to legal lending limits.

3. **Loans secured by documents of title.** Loans secured by bills of lading or warehouse receipts covering readily marketable staples are exempt from the standard limits. This exception allows a bank to make loans to one customer up to 35 percent of capital, if the market value of the staples securing the loans at all times exceeds 115 percent of the loans outstanding. This 35 percent is in addition to the 10 percent and 15 percent general lending limits.

4. **Loans secured by U.S. obligations.** No lending limit applies to loans that are secured fully by the current market value of obligations of the U.S. government, or to transactions secured by obligations guaranteed by the U.S. government, including repurchase agreements, where the purchaser has assured control over or has established its rights to the collateral.

5. **Loans guaranteed by a federal agency.** No lending limit applies to loans covered by a federal unconditional guarantee or commitment if the commitment is payable within 60 days of bank demand.

6. **Loans secured by segregated deposit accounts.** A loan secured by a segregated deposit account in the lending bank will not be subject to any limitation based on capital and surplus.

7. **Loans to financial institutions.** There are no limits on loans that have been approved by the Comptroller of the Currency and are made to any financial institution, receiver, conservator, or superintendent of banks. This exception is intended to apply only in emergency situations.

8. **Discount of installment consumer paper.** A maximum lending limit of 25 percent of the bank's unimpaired capital and surplus applies to loans arising from the discount of installment consumer paper that carries a full recourse endorsement or unconditional guarantee by the person transferring the paper. However, if the bank does full credit work on the underlying consumer paper and the bank certifies in writing that it is relying primarily upon each maker and not on a recourse endorsement, legal lending limits apply only to the makers of the consumer paper.

9. **Loans secured by livestock or dairy cattle.** A 25 percent lending limit applies to loans secured by documents of title covering livestock and dairy cattle when the market value of the underlying livestock is at least equal to 115 percent of the loan at all times, and where an inspection or valuation is made at least annually.

10. **Student Loan Marketing Association obligations.** Loans to the Student Loan Marketing Association (Sallie Mae) are not subject to legal lending limits.

11. **State or political subdivision general obligations.** No lending limit applies to loans to or guaranteed by general obligations of a state or political subdivision.

12. **Intraday overdrafts.** Intraday overdrafts for which payment is received before the bank or thrift closes its books for the calendar day are excluded from lending limit calculations.

13. **Legally unenforceable loans.** A loan, or a portion of the loan, that becomes legally unenforceable and has been charged-off is not a loan or extension of credit.

14. **Additional funds to protect value of collateral.** Additional funds advanced to a borrower for certain expenditures which are necessary to preserve the value of real property collateral are not extensions of credit for purposes of lending limit calculations. However, these advances will be counted for lending limit purposes, if a new loan or credit is extended to the borrower.

Exceptions for Savings Associations

Though the national bank lending limits generally apply to savings associations, several significant exceptions permit savings associations to:

1. Make loans to one borrower for any reason up to $500,000;

2. Make loans to one borrower to develop residential housing units not to exceed the lesser of $30 million or 30 percent of the savings association's capital and surplus if certain requirements are met; and

3. Make loans to one borrower to finance the sale of real property acquired by foreclosure not to exceed 50 percent of the savings association's capital and surplus.

In addition, savings associations may exceed loans to one-borrower limits in furtherance of reasonable, bona fide salvage plans. Because of possible risks to safety and soundness, savings associations are required to contact their appropriate OTS Regional Director before implementing such a plan.

References

Laws:

12 U.S.C. 84
12 U.S.C. 1464(u)

Regulations:

12 CFR 32 (OCC)
12 CFR 560.93 (OTS)

XVIII. Loans Secured by Bank Stock

Introduction and Purpose 144

Loans Secured by Bank's *Own* Stock 144

Loans Secured by *Other* Bank's Stock 144

Reports by Certain Insiders on Loans
    Secured by Stock 145

Stock Held DPC 145

References 145

Introduction and Purpose

No national bank and no state member may make a loan secured by its own stock. If a financial institution makes a loan secured by 25 percent or more of the stock of another financial institution, the lender becomes subject to reporting requirements.

The statutory prohibition is intended to prevent the impairment of the bank's capital and to prevent injury to creditors in the event of the bank's insolvency. The reporting requirement allows for regulatory review of the fairness of the transactions and ensures that those transactions do not adversely affect the safety and soundness of the lending institution.

Loans Secured by Bank's *Own* Stock

Prohibition. All national and state member banks are prohibited from making loans secured by their own stock. Any national or state member bank which acquires its own stock to satisfy a pre-existing debt must dispose of that stock within six months.

Loans Secured by *Other* Bank's Stock

Insured banks, saving associations, and branches and agencies of foreign banks must report the making of any loan secured by more than 25 percent of another institution's stock. If a financial institution and its affiliate together extend credit, they should file a consolidated report.

The report must be filed with the regional or district office of the federal regulatory agency that supervises the institution whose shares secure the loan. It may be submitted in a letter form sufficient to convey the necessary information. The report is required within 30 days of the date that the lender first believed that the security for the credit consisted of more than 25 percent of any class of another insured depository's outstanding stock.

Required Information. The report must include the following information:

- The name of the borrower;

- The amount of the loan; and

- The name of the institution issuing the stock securing the loan and the number of shares securing the loan.

Exceptions. The lender is not required to file if:

- The borrower already has disclosed the required information in a filing with or application to the appropriate federal regulator;

- The borrower has been the owner of record of the stock for a period of one year or more; or

- The stock is of a newly organized institution issued prior to its opening.

Reports by Certain Insiders on Loans Secured by Stock

Each executive officer and director of an insured depository institution or its holding company, the shares of which are not publicly traded, must report annually to the board of directors all loans secured by stock of that institution or holding company.

Stock Held DPC

A bank or savings association may acquire bank stock or bank holding company stock as the result of securing or collecting a debt previously contracted (DPC) without being deemed to be a bank holding company under the Bank Holding Company Act (BHCA). However, the lending institution must dispose of the stock within a two-year period. The Federal Reserve Bank (FRB) may grant requests for up to three one-year extensions. Holding the bank or bank holding company shares beyond the prescribed time limit without FRB approval would constitute a violation of the BHCA if the amount causes the institution to control 25 percent or more of any class of voting shares.

References

Laws:

12 U.S.C. 83
12 U.S.C. 324
12 U.S.C. 1817(j)(9)
12 U.S.C. 1842
12 U.S.C. 3106(a)

Regulations:

12 CFR 7.2019

XIX. Loans to Insiders

Introduction and Purpose 148

Definitions 148

Prohibitions 150

Additional Restrictions and Reports for Executive Officers 152

Maintenance of Records 153

Reports by Banks 153

Disclosures by Banks 153

Restrictions Regarding Correspondent Banks 153

Annual Reports by Executive Officers and Principal Shareholders 154

Reports by Certain Insiders on Loans Secured by Stock 154

Additional Restrictions for Savings Associations 154

References 155

Introduction and Purpose

Sections 22(g) and 22(h) of the Federal Reserve Act, as implemented by the Federal Reserve Board's Regulation O, govern any extension of credit to the following insiders:

- Executive officers;

- Directors;

- Principal shareholders;

- Related interests of an executive officer, director, or principal shareholder; and

- A correspondent bank's executive officers, directors, or principal shareholders or their related interests.

These restrictions are complex and vary depending on the kind of insider and transaction involved. The restrictions historically applied to national banks and state member banks; FDICIA extended them to state nonmember banks and savings associations. For purposes of the discussion in this chapter, all covered institutions are referred to as "banks" or "bank" unless otherwise noted.

FDICIA also made other changes to the restrictions on loans to insiders. These changes, however, do not affect the validity of any loans to insiders lawfully entered into before the effective date of those amendments.

Definitions

Director. An individual who serves on the elected board of directors of the bank, its parent holding company, or any other subsidiary of the bank holding company.

Insider lending restrictions, however, do not apply to a director of the bank's affiliate if:

- The bank — through a by-law or board resolution — excludes him or her from participating in major policy-making functions;

- The assets of the affiliate are less than 10 percent of the assets of the consolidated holding company; and

- The affiliate does not control the bank.

Executive Officer. An individual, regardless of title, who participates or has the authority to participate (other than as a director) in a major policy-making function. Persons with the title of chairman, president, secretary, treasurer, cashier, and every vice president are presumed to be executive officers unless excluded from major policy-making functions by a resolution of the board of directors of the bank or company for which he or she is an officer.

Insider lending restrictions, however, do not apply to an executive officer of the bank's affiliate if:

- The bank — through a by-law or board resolution — excludes him or her from participating in major policy-making functions;

- The assets of the affiliate are less than 10 percent of the assets of the consolidated holding company; and

- The affiliate does not control the bank.

Principal Shareholder. An individual or company that owns or controls more than 10 percent of any class of voting securities of a bank, its parent holding company, or any other subsidiary of the bank holding company. Shares owned by a member of the individual's immediate family are considered to be held by the individual. Bank holding companies are not considered principal shareholders for the purposes of Regulation O.

Related interest. A company, or political or campaign committee, in which a director, executive officer, or principal shareholder has a controlling interest.

Controlling interest. When a person directly or indirectly, or acting in concert with other persons:

- Owns, controls, or has the power to vote 25 percent or more of any class of voting securities of the company; or

- Controls the election of a majority of the directors of the company; or

- Has the power to control management or policies of the company by virtue of:

    a. Being an executive officer or director of the company *and* owning more than 10 percent of any class of voting securities of the company; or

    b. Having more than 10 percent control of voting securities and no other person owning a greater percent of that class.

Extension of credit. The making or renewing of loans, the granting of a credit line (including credit cards over $15,000), endorsements, guarantees, a purchase of securities under repurchase agreement, the issuance of standby letters of credit and overdrafts, and salary advances for more than a 30-day period.

The following transactions are specifically *excluded* from the definition of an extension of credit:

- Arm's-length extensions of credit by financial institutions to third parties where the proceeds of the credit are used to finance the bona fide acquisition of property, goods, or services from an insider or an insider's related interest;

- Discounting of promissory notes, bills of exchange, conditional sales contracts, or similar paper, *without* recourse; and

- Discounting of consumer installment paper with recourse from a dealer that is controlled by an insider, when the institution is primarily relying on the consumer's creditworthiness rather than any guarantee offered by the dealer.

Prohibitions

A bank may extend credit only to a director, executive officer, principal shareholder, or any related interest of that person subject to the following restrictions.

1. **On comparable terms.** Each extension of credit must be involve more than the normal risk of repayment or present other unfavorable features.

   The bank must follow credit underwriting procedures that are no less stringent than those applicable to comparable transactions with persons who are not insiders.

   An insider, however, may take advantage of a benefit or compensation program that is widely available to bank employees, and that does not prefer insiders over other employees.

2. **Prior approval.** Any extension of credit, when aggregated with all other loans or lines of credit to that person or his or her related interests, that (a) exceeds 5 percent of the bank's capital and unimpaired surplus or $25,000, whichever is greater, or (b) exceeds (in any case) $500,000, must be approved in advance by a majority of the entire board of directors of the bank, excluding the interested party.

3. **Overdrafts.** Unless the overdrafts are $1,000 or less and for not more

than five business days and a normal fee is charged, banks are prohibited from paying executive officers' or directors' overdrafts. (Related interests are not covered by this limitation.)

However, an exception is provided if the overdrafts are paid in accordance with:

a. A written, pre-authorized, interest-bearing extension of credit plan specifying a method of repayment; or

b. A written, pre-authorized transfer of funds from another account of the executive officer or director at the bank.

4. **Individual lending limit.** No bank may extend credit to any one of its executive officers, directors, or principal shareholders or any related interest of that person in an amount that, when aggregated with the amount of all other extensions of credit by the bank to that individual and his or her related interests, exceeds the legal lending limit of the bank. (See the Lending Limits section of this *Handbook*.)

5. **Aggregate limit to all insiders.** When all extensions of credit to insiders are aggregated, the total may not exceed the total amount of the bank's unimpaired capital and surplus. *"Unimpaired capital and surplus"* is defined as an insured depository institution's total risk-based capital (Tier I capital plus Tier II capital) together with any balance of its allowance for loan and lease losses not included in Tier II capital, based on the most recent Report of Condition and Income (i.e., Call Report).

FRB regulations, however, allow banks with total deposits of less than $100 million to increase their aggregate amount of insider loans to a level not to exceed two times their unimpaired capital and surplus, provided that the board of directors approves annually the higher limit, and the institution is at least adequately capitalized and has received at least a "satisfactory" rating in the report of its most recent examination.

In addition, transactions deemed to pose "minimal risk" to institutions are exempt from this aggregate limit. These include loans fully secured (and perfected) by:

- U.S. government obligations or obligations fully guaranteed by the U.S. government;

- Commitments and guarantees of a U.S. government department or agency;

- Earmarked deposit accounts at the institution; or

- Certain discounts of installment consumer paper.

6. Knowing receipt of unauthorized loans. An insider may not knowingly receive any unauthorized extensions of credit.

Additional Restrictions and Reports for Executive Officers

Additional restrictions apply to loans made by a bank to its own executive officers. These more stringent restrictions do not apply to an executive officer of the parent holding company or of its other subsidiaries (unless the executive officer is also an executive of the bank).

No bank may extend credit to its officers or to any partnership in which an executive officer holds a partnership interest if the aggregate amount of loans exceeds the greater of 2.5 percent of the bank's capital and unimpaired surplus or $25,000, but in no event more than $100,000 unless the extension of credit is to:

- Finance the education of the executive officer's children; or

- Finance the purchase, construction, maintenance, or improvement of the executive officer's residence, secured by a first lien. Refinancings are also permitted to the extent that proceeds are used to pay off an existing mortgage or for other exempt purposes.

In addition, executive officers may engage in certain "minimal risk" transactions without complying with the limit on general purpose loans. These minimal risk transactions include loans fully secured by:

- U.S. government obligations or obligations fully guaranteed by the U.S. government;

- Commitments and guarantees of a U.S. government department, agency, or instrumentality; or

- Earmarked deposit accounts at the institution.

Executive officers of a bank must report to the bank all indebtedness to any other bank if the aggregate amount of that indebtedness exceeds the lending limit restrictions at their own bank. The report must be filed with the board of directors of the executive's bank within 10 days after exceeding the lending limit, stating the lender's name, the date, amount and purpose of the loan, and the collateral.

Loans to Insiders 153

Maintenance of Records

Insider records. A bank must maintain records to identify all executive officers, directors, principal shareholders, and their related interests and identifying the amounts and terms of all credit extensions to these individuals.

Related interests. The bank must request at least annually that each executive officer, director, and principal shareholder identify their related interests.

Reports by Banks

Call Reports. A national or state member bank must include with each Call Report all extensions of credit made to its own executive officers since the date of the last Call Report. Call Reports also require reporting of the total amount of credit extended to all insiders and their related interests as of the reporting date.

Disclosures by Banks

Public disclosure. If requested in writing, the bank must disclose the names of (1) its principal shareholders, (2) its own executive officers, and (3) their related interests to whom the bank had a loan outstanding at the end of the most recent quarter. Disclosure of names need only be made if aggregate borrowings by that insider are large enough that prior board approval was required in order to make the loan.

The same disclosure is required for loans to executive officers or principal shareholders obtained from a correspondent bank. A record of all such requests for information and their disposition must be maintained for two years from the date of the request.

Restrictions Regarding Correspondent Banks

Banks with a correspondent account relationship are prohibited from extending credit on preferential terms to each other's executive officers, directors, and principal shareholders.

A **correspondent bank** is a bank (or savings association) that maintains one or more correspondent accounts for another bank whose aggregate account balances during a calendar year exceed an average daily figure of $100,000 or 0.5 percent of the other bank's total deposits, whichever is smaller.

Banks also are prohibited from establishing a correspondent account relationship if either of the banks has outstanding a preferential extension of credit to an insider of the other bank.

An extension of credit is considered to be on a preferential basis if:

- It is not made on substantially the same terms, including interest rate and collateral, as those prevailing at the time for comparable transactions with noninsiders; or

- It involves "more than the normal risk of repayment or other unfavorable features."

This restriction extends to savings associations.

Annual Reports by Executive Officers and Principal Shareholders

On or before January 31 of each calendar year, each executive officer and principal shareholder must file a report (FFIEC 004) with the board of directors of his or her bank if that person or related interest had an outstanding extension of credit from a correspondent bank during the previous year. This requirement applies only to the bank's own executive officers, not to those of the bank's parent holding company or the holding company's other subsidiaries.

The report must state (1) the maximum amount of indebtedness during the previous calendar year, (2) the amount of indebtedness outstanding 10 days prior to the report filing, and (3) a description of the loan terms and conditions, including the rate or range of interest rates, original amount and date, maturity date, payment terms, security, and any other unusual terms, if any.

Reports by Certain Insiders on Loans Secured by Stock

Executive officers and directors of any insured depository institution or its holding company, the shares of which are not publicly traded, must report annually to their board of directors all loans secured by stock of such institution or holding company.

Additional Restrictions for Savings Associations

Although savings associations generally are governed by Regulation O, savings associations also are subject to further conflict of interest regulations of the Office of Thrift Supervision. These regulations require directors, officers, or employees of a savings association; persons having the power to direct the management policies of a savings association; and persons owing a fiduciary duty to the savings association to:

- Abstain from advancing their own personal or business interests, or those of others with whom they have a personal or business relationship, at the expense of the savings association;

- Disclose to the board all material nonprivileged information related to an interest in a matter or transaction before the board of directors. This disclosure includes describing the existence, nature, extent of their interests, and the facts surrounding the matter or transaction;

- Refrain from participating in the board's discussion of the matter or transaction; and

- Recuse himself or herself from voting on the matter or transaction if the person is a director.

References

Laws:

12 U.S.C. 375a
12 U.S.C. 375b
12 U.S.C. 1817(k)

Regulations:

12 CFR Part 31 (OCC)
12 CFR Part 215 (Reg. O) (FRB)
12 CFR 337.3 (FDIC)
12 CFR 563.43 and 563.200 (OTS)

XX. Management Interlocks

Introduction and Purpose 158

Applicability 158

General Prohibitions 158

Interlocking Relationships Permitted by Statute 159

Exemptions 160

Change in Circumstances 161

References 161

Introduction and Purpose

Congress enacted the Depository Institution Management Interlocks Act ("Interlocks Act") to increase competition among depository institutions. In general, the Interlocks Act prohibits a management official from serving two nonaffiliated institutions in situations where the management interlock will likely have an adverse effect on competition.

The Interlocks Act is implemented by a regulation issued in 1996 jointly by the FRB, FDIC, OCC, and OTS (the "joint rule").

For a discussion on the limitations imposed by FIRREA on a financial institution's power to appoint certain officials, see the Appointment of Officers and Directors section in this *Handbook*.

Applicability

The joint rule applies to management officials of financial institutions and their affiliates. A "management official" is defined as a:

- Senior executive (including the president, chief executive officer, chief managing official, chief operating officer, chief financial officer, chief lending officer, and chief investment officer);

- Branch manager;

- Director or trustee (including an advisory or honorary director of an institution larger than $100 million); or

- Representative or nominee serving in one of the above capacities.

A "management official," however, does not include anyone who is:

- Involved only in retail merchandising or manufacturing;

- Involved principally in the non-U.S. business of a foreign bank; or

- An officer of a trust company or of a state-chartered institution that does not accept savings deposits or make real estate loans.

General Prohibitions

Under the joint rule, interlocks are prohibited in the following three instances:

Community. A management official of an institution may not serve at the same time as a management official of an unaffiliated institution if the two institutions (or their affiliates) have offices in the same community. A community is defined as the same or adjacent cities, towns, or villages (within 10 road miles).

Relevant Metropolitan Statistical Area (RMSA). A management official of an institution may not serve at the same time as a management official of an unaffiliated institution if the two institutions (or their affiliates) have offices in the same RMSA and *both* institutions have total assets of $20 million or more.

Nationwide. A management official of an institution (or its affiliate) with total assets over $1 billion may not serve at the same time as a management official of an unaffiliated institution with total assets over $500 million, regardless of the location of the two institutions.

Interlocking Relationships Permitted by Statute

Under both the Interlocks Act and the joint rule, prohibitions on interlocks do not apply to the following organizations or their subsidiaries:

- A depository institution that has been placed formally in liquidation, or in the hands of a receiver, conservator, or other official exercising similar functions;

- An Edge or Agreement corporation;

- A credit union being served by a management official of another credit union;

- A depository institution that does not do business in the United States except as incident to its activities outside the United States;

- A state-chartered savings and loan guarantee corporation;

- A Federal Home Loan bank or any other bank organized solely to serve depository institutions or solely to provide securities clearing services for depository institutions and securities companies;

- A depository institution that is closed or in danger of closing and is acquired by another depository institution (this exemption lasts for five years, beginning on the date of acquisition);

- A savings association whose acquisition has been authorized on an emergency basis under the Federal Deposit Insurance Act if the FDIC has given its approval to the interlock;

- A savings association or savings and loan holding company that has issued stock in connection with a qualified stock issuance under the Home Owners' Loan Act; and

- A diversified savings and loan holding company, with respect to a director who serves both the holding company and an unaffiliated depository institution, if the appropriate regulatory agency is notified at least 60 days before dual service begins, and the agency does not disapprove of the service before the end of the 60-day period (the agency may disapprove if the service will have anticompetitive effects or will lead to substantial conflicts of interest or unsafe or unsound practices).

Exemptions

The joint rule allows exemptions in two instances.

Regulatory Standards Exemption

An institution seeking a Regulatory Standards exemption must submit a board resolution certifying that after reasonable efforts, it is unable to locate any other candidate from the relevant community who:

- Has the necessary expertise to serve as a management official;

- Is willing to serve; and

- Is not otherwise prohibited by the Interlocks Act from serving.

Before granting the exemption, the appropriate banking agency must find that:

- The individual is "critical" to the institution's safe and sound operations (critical means important to restoring or maintaining a depository institution's safe and sound operations);

- The interlock will not produce an anticompetitive effect; and

- The management official meets any additional agency requirements.

An interlock permitted under the Regulatory Standards exemption may continue until the appropriate banking agency notifies the affected institutions otherwise. Following notification, a management official may continue to serve for 15 months after the date of the termination order.

Management Consignment Exemption

Under the Management Consignment exemption, the appropriate banking agency may permit an interlock if the interlock will:

- Improve the provision of credit to low-and moderate-income areas;

- Increase the competitive position of a minority- or woman-owned institution;

- Strengthen the management of an institution that has been chartered for less than two years; or

- Strengthen the management of an institution that is in an unsafe or unsound condition.

An interlock permitted under the Management Consignment exemption may continue for a period of two years from the date of approval. The appropriate banking agency may extend this period for one additional two-year period if the institution satisfies one of the above conditions and applies for an extension at least 30 days before the current exemption expires.

Change in Circumstances

The joint rule provides a 15-month grace period for nongrandfathered interlocks that become impermissible under the Interlocks Act due to a change in circumstances. A change in circumstances includes an increase in asset size of an institution, change in the delineation of the RMSA or community, the establishment of an office, an acquisition, merger, consolidation, or any other reorganization of the ownership structure.

References

Laws:

12 U.S.C. 3201 et seq.
12 U.S.C. 1823(k)

Regulations:

12 CFR 26
12 CFR 212 (Regulation L)
12 CFR 348
12 CFR 563f

XXI. Margin Loans

Introduction and Purpose 164

Coverage-Purpose Loan 164

Maximum Loan Value 164

Purpose Statement (Form U-1) 164

Decline in Value of Collateral 165

Single-Credit Rule 165

Withdrawal and Substitutions of Cash or Collateral 166

Special Purpose Loans to Brokers and Dealers 166

Exempted Transactions 166

Proposals 167

References 167

164 Commercial Banking Regulatory Handbook

Introduction and Purpose

Federal Reserve Board Regulation U governs loans to customers for the purpose of buying or carrying stock. Specifically, when loans for the purchase or carrying of margin stocks are collateralized by margin stocks, the value of the loan may not exceed Regulation U's maximum loan value. Currently, the maximum loan value is set at 50 percent of the value of the collateral securing the loan.

Coverage-Purpose Loan

Loans to customers for the purpose of buying or carrying margin stock are referred to as **purpose loans** or **purpose credits.** Regulation U does not apply to nonpurpose loans even if secured by margin stock.

Margin stock is defined to include equity securities traded on a national securities exchange or NASDAQ's National Market System, certain OTC stocks designated by the Federal Reserve Board, bonds, debentures or other securities convertible into such stocks, and mutual funds other than government securities funds.

Extensions of credit include more than formalized loans. Secured overdrafts and letters of credit also are regulated.

Even if margin stock is not pledged, other arrangements — such as a "negative" pledge agreement or safekeeping agreement — may be considered indirect security under Regulation U.

Maximum Loan Value

The **maximum loan value** is set by the Federal Reserve Board as a percentage of market value of the stock securing the loan. Banks may not extend more than the maximum loan value of the margin stock collateral when making purpose loans. Currently, Regulation U sets the maximum loan value at 50 percent.

Purpose Statement (Form U-1)

Whenever a bank extends credit secured directly or indirectly by any margin stock, in any amount exceeding $100,000, the customer is required to execute and sign a purpose statement, Form U-1. This form must be executed even though the credit may be extended for a purpose *other than* purchasing or carrying margin stock. The Form U-1 also must be signed and accepted, in good faith, by an authorized officer of the bank. Good faith requires knowledge of the circumstances surrounding the credit and investigation of any facts that would lead a reasonable person to believe that the stated purpose is not the true purpose of the loan. The bank must retain the form for at least three years after the credit is paid or terminated.

Where the margin stock secures a revolving line of credit or multiple draw agreement, a Form U-1 must be executed at the time the credit arrangement is originally established. If the form is executed at the time the credit is arranged, the credit will be in compliance if the maximum loan value of the collateral at least equals the aggregate amount of funds actually disbursed. A current list of the collateral supporting all credit extended under the agreement must be attached to the Form U-1.

Decline in Value of Collateral

Credit initially extended in compliance with Regulation U does not become noncomplying if (i) the loan value of the collateral decreases due to market fluctuation; (ii) the Federal Reserve changes the maximum loan value; or (iii) nonmargin stock collateral becomes margin stock.

If collateral for a loan subject to the 50 percent collateral requirement of Regulation U declines in value, the bank may decide to continue to carry the loan but may not make any new advances. In addition, no collateral may be released except upon substitution of equivalent collateral. Bank credit policies often require a specified collateral margin to be maintained during the term of the loan.

Single-Credit Rule

Purpose loans to a single customer must be treated as a single credit, and all collateral securing such loans must be considered in determining compliance with Regulation U. Therefore, when a bank is carrying a customer's margin stock secured purpose loan, it may extend unsecured purpose loans to that customer only if the aggregate of purpose loans outstanding does not exceed Regulation U's maximum loan value.

If an unsecured purpose loan is outstanding and a secured purpose loan subsequently is extended, both loans must be aggregated and the total balance must be reduced to comply with the 50 percent maximum loan value requirement before any collateral is released or any new advances are made (other than new advances for which additional collateral is provided).

If the bank extends purpose credit and nonpurpose credit to the same customer, the credits are to be treated as two separate loans. The collateral required for the purpose credit may not be relied upon to secure the nonpurpose credit.

Withdrawal and Substitutions of Cash or Collateral

A withdrawal or substitution of cash or collateral is permitted unless the action will cause the credit to exceed the maximum loan value of the credit or increase the amount by which the credit exceeds the maximum loan value of the collateral. The maximum loan value for this purpose is to be calculated as of the date of the substitution or withdrawal.

Special Purpose Loans to Brokers and Dealers

The following special purpose loans may be extended to broker-dealers without complying with the restrictions above:

- Hypothecation loans;
- Temporary advances in payment against delivery transactions;
- Loans for securities in transit or transfer;
- Intraday loans;
- Arbitrage loans;
- Market maker and specialist loans;
- Underwriter loans;
- Emergency loans;
- Capital contribution loans; and
- Loans to specialists.

Brokers and dealers seeking to apply this exception must execute written notice certifying the purpose of each loan. The lending bank or savings association must accept the notice in good faith.

Exempted Transactions

The following types of transactions are not subject to Regulation U:

- Loans to any bank;

- Loans to any foreign banking institution;

- Loans made outside the U.S. (negotiation, signing and disbursal of funds should take place outside of the U.S. to ensure that the loan meets the exemption);

- Loans to an ESOP;

- Loans to customers, other than a broker-dealer, to temporarily finance the purchase or sale of securities for prompt delivery if the credit is to be repaid in the ordinary course of business upon completion of the transaction;

- Loans against securities transit, with certain exceptions; and

- Loans to enable a customer to meet emergency expenses not reasonably foreseeable. (The opportunity to realize monetary gain or avoid loss does not fit this exemption.)

Proposals

> Except change in Regulation U's reporting and purpose statement requirements. The Federal Reserve's April 1998, advanced notice of proposed rulemaking has generated favorable comments. Federal Reserve officials hope to adopt many of the proposed changes as a final rule by the year end 1998.

In January 1998, the Federal Reserve Board proposed changes to the reporting and registration requirements and loan value regulations contained in Regulation U. The new rule, if adopted, would make the requirements for purpose statements uniform, eliminate unnecessary reporting burdens, and change the registration requirements for lenders, other than brokers or dealers who do not extend purpose credit. Potential changes to the loan value regulations include: modifying the prohibition on loan value for OTC options, creating additional exclusions from the definition of margin stocks for mutual funds, and extending Regulation U-exempted transactions to nonbank lenders. Comments were due in April 1998, suggesting that a final regulation might be issued in the summer of 1998.

References

Laws:

    15 U.S.C. 78a et seq.

Regulations:

    12 CFR 221 (Reg. U) (FRB)

XXII. Political Contributions

Introduction and Purpose 170

Prohibitions 170

Definitions 170

Exceptions 170

Penalties 171

References 171

Introduction and Purpose

The Federal Election Campaign Act prohibits *any* bank or savings association from contributing funds to political candidates or parties in *federal elections*. For *federally chartered institutions*, the prohibition on campaign contributions is extended to cover *state and local elections* as well. While these prohibitions prevent financial institutions from influencing elections by underwriting friendly candidates, they also insulate institutions from political pressure to make unwanted or unsafe loans.

Prohibitions

Federally chartered institutions. National banks and other federally chartered institutions are prohibited from making any contribution or expenditure in connection with any election for *any* political office, including local, state, or federal offices.

State chartered institutions. State-chartered banks and savings associations, as well as all corporations, are prohibited under the Act from making any contribution or expenditure in connection with any election for federal office. Such institutions may make contributions or expenditures for state and local elections to the extent permitted by state or local law.

Definitions

Federal office means the office of President or Vice President of the United States, Senator or Representative in, or Delegate or Resident Commissioner to, the Congress of the United States.

Contribution or expenditure includes any direct or indirect purchase, payment, distribution, loan, advance, deposit or gift of money or service, or anything of value, made to any candidate, campaign committee, or political party or organization.

Exceptions

The Federal Election Campaign Act provides the following exceptions:

Loans or extensions of credit. A bank may loan money to a candidate or party as long as the loan is in the ordinary course of business and in accordance with applicable banking laws. Many states have laws relating to political loans.

PACs. A bank can establish, administer, and solicit contributions for a political action committee (PAC), which is a separate, segregated fund established for political purposes. Because of the requirements and limitations applicable to PACs, the advice of legal counsel always should be sought prior to its establishment.

Penalties

In addition to fines imposed on the institution, any director or officer who consents to any contribution or expenditure by the bank in violation of the Act is subject to fine or imprisonment or both.

References

Laws:

2 U.S.C. 441b

Regulations:

11 CFR Parts 100 and 114
(Federal Election Commission)

XXIII. Real Estate Appraisals

Introduction and Purpose 174

Transactions Covered 174

Transactions Requiring an Appraisal 174

Nonappraisal Evaluations 176

Transactions Requiring a Certified Appraiser 176

Transactions Requiring Either a Certified *or* Licensed Appraiser 177

Certification and Licensing Requirements 177

Appraisal Standards 177

Appraiser Independence 177

References 178

Introduction and Purpose

The federal banking agencies have issued uniform appraisal standards for financial institutions' real estate related transactions. These standards specify those transactions requiring an appraisal and mandate the level of the appraiser's credentials.

The standards generally require appraisals in all real estate related financial transactions exceeding $250,000. Complex transactions and all transactions exceeding $1 million require the services of a state certified appraiser. Appraisals for noncomplex transactions under $1 million may be provided by either a state certified or state licensed appraiser.

The use of state certified and licensed appraisers is intended to assure that all appraisals will be in writing, in accordance with uniform standards, and performed by competent individuals whose professional conduct is subject to appropriate supervision.

Transactions Covered

The appraisal requirements apply to any **real estate related financial transaction** entered into after August 9, 1990.

The regulations define **real estate** to include any identified parcel or tract of land, with improvements, easements, rights of way, undivided or future interests, or similar rights. If the transaction does not involve the associated land, regulations expressly exclude from this definition all mineral rights, timber rights, growing crops, water rights, and other interest severable from the land.

A **real estate related financial transaction** means any transaction involving:

- The sale, lease, purchase, investment in, or exchange of real property, including interests in property, or its financing;

- The refinancing of real property or interests in real property; or

- The use of real property or interests in property as security for a loan or investment, including mortgage-backed securities.

Transactions Requiring an Appraisal

An appraisal is required for all real estate related transactions *unless* the transaction is covered by one of the following exceptions:

- **Below threshold.** The transaction value is $250,000 or less.

- **Abundance of caution.** A lien on real estate has been taken as collateral in an abundance of caution and the loan is well supported by the borrower's income or other collateral.

- **Unsecured loans.** The transaction is not secured by real estate.

- **Liens for purposes other than real estate's value.** A lien on real estate has been taken for purposes other than the real estate's value, for example, liens taken against real estate to protect the creditor's rights to, or control over, collateral other than real estate.

- **Certain business loans.** The transaction is a business loan that:

    a. Has a transaction value of $1 million or less; and

    b. Is not dependent on the sale of, or rental income derived from, *any* real estate as the primary source of repayment. This includes income or proceeds from all other real estate not covered by the lien.

- **Leases.** The transaction is a lease of real estate, unless the lease is the economic equivalent of a purchase or sale of the leased real estate.

- **Renewals, refinancings, and other subsequent transactions.** The transaction involves the existing extension of credit from the same lender provided that either:

    a. The transaction does not involve the advancement of new monies, other than funds necessary to cover reasonable closing costs; or

    b. Any advancement of new monies does not threaten the institution's real estate collateral protection.

- **Transactions involving real estate notes.** The transaction involves the purchase, sale, investment in, exchange of, or extension of credit secured by a loan or interest in a loan, pooled loans, or interests in real property, including mortgage-backed securities *provided that* each loan, interest in a loan, pooled loan, or real property interest met appraisal requirements applicable at the time of its origination.

- **Insured or guaranteed by the U.S. government or a G.S.E.** The transaction is insured or guaranteed by a U.S. government agency or a U.S. government sponsored enterprise.

- **Qualified for sale to the U.S. government or a G.S.E.** The transaction either:

    a. Qualifies for sale to a U.S. government agency or U.S. government sponsored enterprise; or

    b. Involves a residential real estate transaction in which the appraisal conforms to FNMA or FHLMC appraisal standards.

- **Institutions as fiduciary.** The institution is acting in a fiduciary capacity and is not required to obtain an appraisal under other law.

- **Determined not necessary.** Federal regulators have determined that the services of an appraiser are not necessary in order to protect public policy interests or the safety and soundness of the institution.

Nonappraisal Evaluations

For transactions that do not require appraisal because they (i) fall below the $250,000 threshold level, (ii) qualify for the exemption for certain business loans, or (iii) qualify for the exemption for renewals, refinancings, and other subsequent transactions, financial institutions must complete a nonappraisal evaluation of real estate value. The nonappraisal evaluation provides a general estimate of the value of real estate without meeting the detailed requirements of an appraisal.

The federal regulators suggest that the evaluation be conducted by an individual who has real estate-related training or experience relevant to the type of property. The evaluation should be documented fully. The evaluation should be in writing, signed and dated, and include the preparer's name and address. It should describe the property, give its location, and discuss its use. The evaluation also should include any of the evaluator's calculations, supporting assumptions, and, if used, a discussion of comparable properties.

Transactions Requiring a Certified Appraiser

State certified appraisers are required to be used for the following real estate-related financial transactions:

1. All transactions of $1 million or more;

2. All nonresidential (i.e., not relating to one- to four-family residential properties) transactions of $250,000 or more; and

Real Estate Appraisals

3. All complex residential transactions of $250,000 or more. The appraisal of a one- to four-family residential property generally is presumed not to be complex. The regulated institution is responsible for determining whether an appraisal is complex.

Transactions Requiring Either a Certified *or* Licensed Appraiser

All transactions requiring an appraisal, but not requiring a state certified appraiser, may utilize the services of either a state certified or a state licensed appraiser.

Certification and Licensing Requirements

State certified appraisers must meet the minimum certification criteria established by the Appraisal Foundation, and pass a written exam. State licensed appraisers need only satisfy state licensing requirements.

To provide federal oversight of the state appraiser authorization process, Congress has established an Appraisal Subcommittee of the Federal Financial Institutions Examination Council. In addition to its monitoring role, the Subcommittee must maintain a national registry of certified and licensed appraisers eligible to perform appraisals on federally related transactions.

Appraisal Standards

Each of the federal bank regulatory agencies has adopted minimum standards for the performance of appraisals made in connection with federally related transactions. All appraisers must complete written appraisal reports following appraisal standards of the Appraisal Standards Board.

Appraiser Independence

Staff Appraisers

If a staff appraiser prepares an appraisal, that appraiser must be independent of the lending, investment, and collection functions, and not involved, except as an appraiser, in the federally related transaction. In addition, the appraiser must have no direct or indirect interest in the subject property.

Fee Appraisers

If a fee appraiser prepares an appraisal, the appraiser shall be engaged directly by the financial institution or its agent and have no direct or indirect interest in the property.

A financial institution also may accept an appraisal that was prepared by an appraiser engaged directly by another financial services institution, if:

a. The appraiser has no financial or other interest in the property or the transaction; and

b. The institution determines that the appraisal conformed to the regulatory requirements.

References

Laws:

12 U.S.C. 3331 et seq.

Regulations:

12 CFR Part 34, Subpart C (OCC)
12 CFR Part 225.61-.67 (FRB)
12 CFR Part 323 (FDIC)
12 CFR Part 564 (OTS)

XXIV. Real Estate Lending Standards

Introduction and Purpose 180

Guideline Applicability 180

Policy Formulation 180

Supervisory LTV Limits 181

Exceptions and Exclusions 182

Supervisory Review 183

References 183

Introduction and Purpose

The four regulatory agencies (OCC, OTS, FDIC, and FRB) have issued identical guidelines that establish real estate lending standards for insured depositories. The guidelines require each bank or thrift making real estate loans to adopt a written policy setting its strategy, limits, and procedures for real estate credit risk taking and management. This policy is to be reviewed and approved annually by the institution's board of directors.

Guideline Applicability

The guidelines define real estate lending as credit secured by liens or interests in real estate, or that is extended to finance permanent improvements to real estate. They explicitly apply to:

- National banks;

- State banks that are FDIC insured;

- U.S. branches of foreign banks that are FDIC insured; and

- Savings associations, their operating subsidiaries, and other controlled subsidiaries not subject to the "deduction from the regulatory capital rule."

These guidelines do not apply to the following entities:

- Bank holding companies and their nonbank subsidiaries; and

- Savings association subsidiaries subject to the "deduction from regulatory capital rule."

While the guidelines do not apply directly to uninsured branches or agencies of foreign banks, examiners are likely to rely on the guidelines when reviewing branch or agency credit portfolios.

Policy Formulation

The regulators expect the board of directors of each institution to adopt and annually review written policies governing real estate lending. These policies should match the institution's strategy, limits, and procedures to the following internal and external factors:

- Its size and financial condition;

- Its expertise;

- Its markets;
- Economic conditions;
- Concentrations of risks; and
- Other applicable regulations, including CRA.

These policies should:

> Regulatory guidelines require real estate lending policies to be approved annually by ther board of directors.

- Identify the geographic areas in which the institution will consider lending;
- Set limits for real estate loans by type and geographic market;
- Identify the acceptable types of real estate loans, terms, and conditions;
- Establish prudent underwriting standards that are clear and measurable, including loan to value (LTV) limits that are consistent with the supervisory guidelines shown below;
- Establish loan origination and approval procedures, both generally and by size and type of loan, and for the exception loans;
- Establish loan administration procedures, including documentation, disbursement, collateral inspection, collection, and loan review;
- Monitor economic and market conditions, and factor them into strategic and lending decisions;
- Monitor and report timely and adequately to the board of directors the condition and composition of the loan portfolio, including policy exceptions; and
- Establish real estate appraisal and evaluation programs as part of portfolio management.

Supervisory LTV Limits

The guidelines list considerations and limits that the agencies will expect to find when reviewing an institution's real estate lending policies. Of special interest are the supervisory LTV limits. The regulators believe that lending policies should not incorporate LTVs exceeding the following ratios:

182 Commercial Banking Regulatory Handbook

Loan Type	LTV Limit
Raw Land	65%
Land Development	75%
Construction:	
Nonresidential	80%
1- to 4- Family Residential	85%
Improved Property (except loans on owner-occupied 1- to 4-family property)	85%
Owner-occupied 1- to 4-family and home equity	**

** For a permanent mortgage or home equity loan on owner occupied 1- to 4-family residential property with an LTV 90 percent at origination, private mortgage insurance or readily marketable collateral should cover the portion of the loan greater than 80 percent LTV.

Exceptions and Exclusions

The guidelines permit a bank or savings association to make real estate loans exceeding the suggested LTV ratios up to an aggregate amount not exceeding 100 percent of the institution's total risk-based capital, with a 30 percent sub-limit for nonresidential real estate related credit. All exceptions $250,000 or larger are to be reported individually to the board of directors. All others are to be reported to the board in aggregates, at least quarterly.

Other transactions excluded from the LTV are:

- Loans guaranteed or insured by the U.S. government or its agencies, or by the full faith and credit of its agencies, where the "guaranty" or "credit" is at least equal to the excess of the loan over the LTV limit;

- Loans that are renewed, refinanced, or restructured without the advancement of new funds (except for reasonable closing costs);

- Loans that are renewed, refinanced, or restructured in connection with a work-out situation, either with or without the advancement of new funds, where the extension is done in accordance with safe and sound practices, and is documented to maximize recovery;

- Loans that facilitate the sale of real estate acquired by the lender in the course of collecting a debt previously contracted in good faith;

- Loans where real property is taken as an abundance of caution, and the value of the real property is low relative to the aggregate value of all other collateral;

- Loans, such as working capital loans, where the lender does not rely principally on real estate as security and the extension of credit is not used to acquire, develop, or construct permanent improvements on real property;

- Loans for the purpose of financing permanent improvements to real property, but not secured by the property, if such security interest is not required by prudent underwriting practice; and

- Loans that are to be sold promptly after origination, without recourse, to a financially responsible third party.

Supervisory Review

In the course of their examinations, the agencies will be assessing real estate loan policies and practices against the guidelines, the nature and scope of the institution's real estate lending activities, its financial condition, the quality of its management, staff expertise and controls, and market conditions.

References

Laws:

12 U.S.C. 371(a) and 1828(o)

Regulations:

12 CFR Part 34 (OCC), Subpart D
12 CFR Part 208 (FRB), Appendix C
12 CFR Part 365 (FDIC)
12 CFR 545.30 and 560.100 (OTS)

XXV. Real Estate Ownership

Introduction and Purpose 186

General Limitation 186

Bank Premises 186

Future Expansion 187

Finance Leases 187

Other Real Estate Owned (OREO) 188

Disposal of OREO 188

OREO Holding Period 189

Improvements to OREO 189

OREO Accounting Requirements 190

OREO Appraisals 190

References 190

186 Commercial Banking Regulatory Handbook

Introduction and Purpose

Federal law severely limits the power of national banks and savings associations to purchase, hold, and convey real estate. Most states have similar laws restricting real estate activities of state-chartered banks. OCC also regulates a national bank's holding and administration of foreclosed real estate. This chapter focuses primarily on the federal law applicable to national banks.

The federal limitations on real estate activities were designed to protect the safety of customers' deposits by preventing real estate speculation by banks, to rechannel bank capital throughout the community, and to prevent mass accumulation of property by banks.

General Limitation

A national bank may obtain interests in real estate only for the following reasons:

- **Bank Premises.** To conduct its own banking business;

- **Collateral.** As collateral for loans, including the holding of a mortgage or deed of trust;

- **Satisfaction of debts.** To satisfy a previously contracted debt through foreclosure, purchase, or other conveyance; or

- **Trustee.** As a trustee or other fiduciary strictly for the benefit of someone else.

Bank Premises

A national bank may purchase or lease real estate used in conducting its banking business, such as:

- Property used by the bank itself, including

    a. Teller lobbies and office space,

    b. Data processing or operating centers,

    c. Storage space,

    d. Maintenance facilities, and

    e. Property for future expansion;

- Property used by bank customers or employees including

    a. Parking lots,

    b. Residences for employees on temporary assignments or in remote or foreign locations,

    c. Residences of transferred employees whose sale would cause a loss to the employee, and

    d. Temporary lodging whose cost is tax deductible; and

- Lease financing of public facilities.

A bank has limited authority to lease its real estate to others. For example, a bank constructing its own office and bank facilities on valuable downtown real estate may realize the full value of that real estate by erecting a skyscraper and leasing out the portions of the building not used by the bank.

Future Expansion

OCC expects a national bank acquiring real estate for future expansion normally to begin using it within five years. If not occupied by the bank within one year, the bank's board of directors should approve, or authorize a bank official to approve, a definitive plan for its use.

When a bank ceases to use real estate as bank premises, or decides not to use real estate acquired for future expansion, the property should be transferred to **other real estate owned** (OREO). The property then becomes subject to the disposal and other OREO limitations.

Finance Leases

OCC has interpreted the federal statutes to prohibit a national bank from financing a customer's acquisition of real estate through a lease financing arrangement (i.e., acquiring the desired real estate and leasing it to the customer). This interpretation differs from that governing personal property, which a bank is permitted to acquire and lease to a customer. This distinction sometimes causes difficulty when a bank undertakes lease financing for a plant or other facility that consists of both real and personal property.

Other Real Estate Owned (OREO)

A bank may acquire real estate in satisfaction of a debt previously contracted in good faith, whether or not that real estate was collateral for the debt. Real estate so acquired typically is the principal source of a bank's OREO.

OREO consists of real estate acquired by a bank through:

- Purchases at sales under judgments, decrees, or mortgages when the property was security for debts previously contracted;

- Conveyances in satisfaction of debts previously contracted;

- Purchases to secure debts previously contracted;

- Termination of use as banking premises; or

- Abandonment of plans to use real estate acquired for future expansion for banking premises.

Disposal of OREO

OCC's regulation provides that an institution may dispose of OREO by entering into a transaction that:

- Receives sales treatment under GAAP;

- Is insured by the U.S. Government or one of its agencies, or is a loan eligible for purchase by a federally sponsored instrumentality (e.g., Federal National Mortgage Corporation);

- Is a land contract or a contract for deed;

- Disposes of a capitalized or operating lease by obtaining an assignment or a coterminous sublease;

- Uses the real estate for its own bank premises or transfers it to a subsidiary or affiliate for use in their business; or

- Results in the institution receiving at least 10 percent of the total sales price in cash, principal and interest payments, and private mortgage insurance, measured in accordance with generally accepted accounting principles (GAAP).

OCC also recognizes noncoterminous subleases as a permissible way to dispose of leased premises held as OREO. Banks may enter into these leases in good faith without being cited for a violation of law. The divestiture period is suspended for the duration of the noncoterminous sublease and begins running again upon termination of the lease. A bank may not enter into a sublease for the purpose of real estate speculation. If OCC discovers such speculation, the bank may be required to take immediate steps to dispose of the lease.

OREO Holding Period

A bank may not hold OREO for longer than five years.

The Comptroller of the Currency may approve a bank's application to extend the five-year holding period, but not to exceed an additional five years, if:

- The bank has made a good faith attempt to dispose of the real estate within the five-year period; or

- Disposal within the five-year period would be detrimental to the bank.

The holding period begins on the date that (1) ownership of the property is originally transferred to an institution, (2) relocation from former banking premises to new banking premises is complete, or (3) a decision is made not to use real estate acquired for future expansion, and ends on the date that the institution disposes of the property. For foreclosed property subject to a redemption period under state law, the holding period begins when the redemption period expires.

A bank must maintain current documentation reflecting its continuing and diligent efforts to dispose of each parcel of OREO. If at any time before the end of the holding period the bank can recover the amount of the original loan plus additional advances and other costs related to the loan or the parcel of OREO, it should promptly dispose of the parcel.

Improvements to OREO

Normal costs of property management — such as taxes, insurance, maintenance expenses, and managerial fees — should be expensed by the banks and do *not* require regulatory approval. A national bank may expend funds to complete a development or improvement project if the bank will reduce the shortfall between the parcel's market value and recorded investment amount, and if the expenditures are not for speculation. National banks will be required to notify their supervisory office and provide adequate documentation, if the sum of the improvement or development plan's costs, the current recorded investment amount, and any prior liens exceeds 10 percent of the bank's capital and surplus. The national bank may carry out its plan on the 31st day after filing this notification (or sooner if notified by the OCC), subject to any limitations imposed by the supervisory office.

Notification is not required for re-fitting an existing building for new tenants, or for normal repairs and maintenance costs incurred to protect the value of the collateral.

OREO Accounting Requirements

A bank is generally required to account for sales of OREO according to generally accepted accounting principles (GAAP). Specific accounting guidance is provided in the Call Report instructions to Schedule RC-M.

OREO Appraisals

When a property is transferred to OREO, its market value must be substantiated. Appraisals are necessary only when the property's loan balance or net book value exceeds $250,000, and the property has not been previously appraised. When an appraisal is not required, banks may substantiate market value by some other prudent evaluation method.

In addition, banks must establish a collateral evaluation policy that monitors the value of each parcel of OREO throughout its holding period.

References

Laws:

    12 U.S.C. 29
    12 U.S.C. 1464(c)
    12 U.S.C. 1831e(c)

Regulations:

    12 CFR 7.1000
    12 CFR Part 34, Subparts C and E (OCC)
    12 CFR 560.172 (OTS)

XXVI. Reserves on Deposits

Introduction and Purpose 192

Affected Institutions 192

Definitions 192

Reserve Requirements 193

Maintenance of Reserves 193

Reporting of Deposits 194

Computation of Reserves 195

References 196

Introduction and Purpose

The Federal Reserve Board's Regulation D sets uniform reserve requirements on all depository institutions that maintain transaction accounts, nonpersonal time deposits, or Eurocurrency liabilities. Reserve requirements are one of the means by which the Federal Reserve Board conducts monetary policy.

The opportunity cost of holding reserve balances, which yield no return, provides incentive to depository institutions to minimize their holdings of excess reserves.

Affected Institutions

Regulation D applies to all depository institutions that maintain transaction accounts, nonpersonal time deposits, or Eurocurrency liabilities. It also applies to U.S. branches and agencies of foreign banks with total worldwide consolidated assets in excess of $1 billion and to Edge Act and Agreement corporations.

Definitions

Depository institutions include any federal- or state-chartered depository institution that is federally insured or that is eligible for federal deposit insurance.

Transaction accounts are deposits from which the depositor is permitted to make transfers or withdrawals by negotiable order or check, telephone, or similar device for making third-party payments. They include:

- Demand deposits;

- NOW accounts;

- Share draft accounts;

- Savings accounts with automatic transfer service capabilities;

- Savings accounts that permit more than three withdrawals to third parties per month;

- Money market deposit accounts (MMDAs) for which the bank permits, or does not prevent, the number of pre-authorized withdrawals to exceed the regulatory limitations; and

- Time deposits for which the bank does not impose at least the required minimum early withdrawal penalties.

Nonpersonal time deposits are time deposits (including savings accounts or MMDAs that do not qualify as transaction accounts) that are:

- Held by depositors who are not natural persons; and

- Transferable and held by one or more natural persons.

For a time deposit to be considered nontransferable for the purposes of the regulation, the deposit document must have, on its face, a statement that it is not transferable or that it is transferable only on the books of, or with the permission of, the depository institution.

Eurocurrency liabilities are defined as net borrowings from related foreign offices, loans to United States residents made by related foreign offices, and assets held by related foreign affiliates acquired from domestic offices.

Reserve Requirements

For 1998, the Federal reserve has decreased the low reserve tranche from $49.3 million to $47.8 million. The Fed increased to $4.7 million the deposits exempt from reserves.

The following reserve requirements currently are prescribed for all affected depository institutions:

Category	Reserve Requirement
Net transaction accounts $0 to 47.8 million . . . Over $47.8 million . .	3 percent of amount $1,434,000 plus 10 percent of amount over $47.8 million
Nonpersonal time deposits	0 percent
Eurocurrency liabilities	0 percent

The amount of transaction deposits subject to the 3 percent reserve ratio is adjusted each calendar year. This adjustment is known as the low reserve tranche adjustment.

To provide reserve requirement relief to small depository institutions, for 1998, Regulation D exempts the first $4.7 million in reservable liabilities of each depository institution from reserve requirements. This exemption amount is revised annually.

Maintenance of Reserves

Depository institutions may hold reserves in the form of (1) vault cash, (2) a balance maintained directly with the Federal Reserve Bank, or (3) a pass-through account at a correspondent bank that is a member of the Federal Reserve.

Nonmember depository institutions may utilize the following institutions as a pass-through correspondent:

- Any institution that maintains required reserve balances at a Federal Reserve Bank;

- Federal Home Loan Banks;

- National Credit Union Administration Central Liquidity Facility; or

- Any institution that has been authorized by the Board to pass through required reserve balances.

Reporting of Deposits

Reporting requirements vary depending on the type of institution, the institution's exemption status, total deposits, and source of funds.

Weekly Reporting

The following institutions are required to file a Report of Transaction Accounts, Other Deposits and Vault Cash (Form FR 2900) on a weekly basis with their Federal Reserve Bank:

1. Institutions with reservable liabilities in excess of $4.7 million (nonexempt institutions) that have total deposits of $78.9 million or more (the nonexempt "deposit cutoff level");

2. U.S. branches and agencies of foreign banks; and

3. Edge and Agreement corporations.

Quarterly Reporting

Institutions with reservable liabilities in excess of $4.7 million that have total deposits of less than $78.9 million must file the FR 2900 quarterly.

Institutions with reservable liabilities less than or equal to $4.7 million (the "exemption level") and with total deposits of $50.7 million or more (the exempt "deposit cutoff "level) must file the Quarterly Report of Selected Deposits, Vault Cash and Reservable Liabilities (Form FR 2910q).

Annual Reporting

Institutions with reservable liabilities less than or equal to $4.7 million that have total deposits of $4.7 million or more but less than $50.7 million must file the Annual Report of Total Deposits and Reservable Liabilities (Form FR 2910a).

Institutions that obtain funds from non-U.S. sources or that have foreign branches or international banking facilities are required to file a Report of Certain Eurocurrency Transactions (FR 2950/2951) on the same frequency as Form FR 2900.

As required by the Federal Reserve Act, the Federal Reserve, prior to December 31 of each year, adjusts the nonexempt and the exempt deposit cutoff levels. The Federal Reserve may also adjust the exemption level annually.

Computation of Reserves

Effective July 30, 1998, the Federal Reserve has changed the system of contemporaneous reserve requirements for weekly reporters to a system of lagged reserves. Under the new system, an institution must determine its required reserves by applying the reserve ratio to the amounts of transaction accounts, nonpersonal time deposits, and Eurocurrency liabilities held.

Reserve needs are figured for a two week period on a 17-day lagged basis.

Specifically, the amount that a bank must maintain in transaction account reserves is computed on the basis of daily average balances of deposit liabilities during a 14-day period ending every second Monday (the "computation period"). The institution must maintain the reserve balance with the Federal Reserve during a 14-day period (the "maintenance period"), which begins on the third Thursday following the end of a given computation period. The maintenance period will begin 30 days after the beginning of a reserve computation period.

In determining the amount of the required reserve balance, the institution must deduct its daily average vault cash during the computation period from the amount of its required reserves.

The Federal Reserve allows banks to carry a reserve excess or deficiency into the following two-week reserve period. Thus, a bank can miss its reserve requirements by up to 4 percent on either side and be allowed to carry this position to meet or increase its new reserve requirement in the next two-week period. Any carryover not offset during the next period may not be carried forward to subsequent periods.

TABLE 1

SUN	MON	TUES	WED	THURS	FRI	SAT
13	*14*	*15*	*16*	*17*	*18*	*19*
20	*21*	*22*	*23*	*24*	*25*	*26*
27	*28*	29	30	1	2	3
4	5	6	7	8	9	10
11	12	13	14	15 •••• ★★★★	16 •••• ★★★★	17 •••• ★★★★
18 •••• ★★★★	19 •••• ★★★★	20 •••• ★★★★	21 •••• ★★★★	22 •••• ★★★★	23 •••• ★★★★	24 •••• ★★★★
25 •••• ★★★★	26 •••• ★★★★	27 •••• ★★★★	28 •••• ★★★★	29	30	31

▨ Lagged computation period for nontransaction amounts and Eurocurrency liabilities.

•••• Lagged computation period for vault cash.

★★★★ Lagged reserve maintenance period.

References

Laws:

12 U.S.C. 461

Regulations:

12 CFR Part 204 (Reg. D) (FRB)

XXVII. Tying Provisions

Introduction and Purpose 198

Prohibited Tying Arrangements 198

Exceptions 199

Private Lawsuits 199

References 200

Introduction and Purpose

A bank may not require a borrower, as a condition of obtaining a loan, to acquire nontraditional services or products, such as credit life insurance or brokerage services, from the bank itself.

A bank may, however, demand that the borrower:

- Obtain another loan, discount, deposit, or trust service (this is known as the "traditional bank product exception") from the bank or an affiliate; or

- Provide to an affiliate some additional credit, property, or service that the bank itself could require.

Thus the bank may insist on such common loan terms as a compensating balance or an escrow account and may engage in linked promotions, such as offering free checking accounts to borrowers.

The purpose of the anti-tying provision is to protect small independent businesspeople and others from unfair and predatory business practices by banks.

The provision applies to all insured banks. Similar restrictions are applicable to saving associations.

Prohibited Tying Arrangements

A bank generally may not extend credit, lease or sell property, furnish any service, or fix or vary the consideration on any of the following conditions or requirements:

- That the customer obtains some additional credit, property, or service from the bank other than a loan, discount, deposit, or trust service;

- That the customer obtains some additional credit, property, or service from its bank holding company, or from any other subsidiary of the bank holding company;

- That the customer provides some additional credit, property, or service to the bank, other than those related to and usually provided in connection with a loan, discount, deposit, or trust service;

- That the customer provides some additional credit, property, or service to its bank holding company or to any other subsidiary of the bank holding company; or

- That the customer may not obtain some credit, property, or service from a competitor of the bank other than by a condition or requirement that the bank may reasonably impose to assure the soundness of the credit.

Exceptions

The Federal Reserve Board permits certain exceptions to the anti-tying prohibitions if all of the products involved in the tying arrangement are available separately for purchase. In February 1997, the FRB rescinded the application of the special bank anti-tying rules to bank holding companies and their non-bank subsidiaries. The Board determined that the general antitrust laws could address any potential competitive problems. The exceptions to the anti-tying provisions now apply solely to banks. The term "bank" includes U.S. branches or agencies of foreign banks and their commercial lending subsidiaries.

Banks may vary the consideration for any product or package of products based on the customer maintaining a combined minimum balance in certain products, specified by the bank as "eligible products" if:

- The bank offers deposits and all deposits are eligible products; and

- Balances in deposits count at least as much as nondeposit products toward the minimum balance.

Banks may engage in any transactions with a foreign customer, that is, a customer who is:

- A corporation, business, or person (other than an individual) that is incorporated, chartered, or otherwise organized outside the United States and has its principal place of business outside the United States; or

- A citizen of a foreign country and a non-U.S. resident.

Private Lawsuits

A person "injured in his business or property" may sue the bank for treble damages or an injunction or both. Any such lawsuit must be brought within four years of the event.

References

Laws:

12 U.S.C. 1464(q)
12 U.S.C. 1971 - 1978

Regulations:

12 CFR 225.7

Index

A

Abundance of caution, 175
Accountant, independent public (IPA), 24
"Accounting by Creditors for Impairment of a Loan," 53
"Accounting for Mortgage Servicing Rights," 55
"Accounting for Transfers and Servicing of Financial Assets and Extinguishments of Liabilities," 51
Accounting standards
    general requirements, 26
    introduction and purpose, 22
    laws and regulations references, 26
    See also Audits and attestation
Adequately capitalized institutions, 38–39, 40, 49, 71
Adjusted add-on amount (Anet), 65
Administrative costs, international loans, 122
Advance funds, contractual commitment to, 136–39
    definition of, 133
Advanced funds, 140
"Affiliate," definition of, 10
Affiliate obligations, responsibility for, 15
Affiliate transactions
    capital percentage limitations, 12
    collateral requirements, 12–13
    covered affiliates, 10, 14
    covered transactions, 11, 14–15
    establishment of control, 10–11
    exempt affiliates, 11
    introduction and purpose, 10
    laws and regulations references, 16
    purchase from affiliate as underwriter, 15
    purchase of low-quality assets, 13
    restrictions, 15
        exemptions to Section 23A, 13–14
        for savings associations, 15–16
Agency fees, international loans, 123
Aggregate limit, to insiders, 151
Agreement and Edge corporations, 110, 111, 112–14
    foreign investment activities, 116–21
    prudential restrictions on, 115–16
    reserve on deposits (Regulation D), 192
Alarm systems, 32–33
Allocated transfer risk reserve (ATRR), 121–22
Allowance for loan and lease losses ("ALLL"), 83
Amortizing fees, international loans, 122

Annual Report of Total Deposits and Reservable Liabilities (Form FR 2910a), 195
Annual reports
    filed with the FDIC, 22–23
    insider loans and, 154
Appointment of officers and directors
    affected institutions, 18
    agency action, 19
    introduction and purpose, 18
    laws and regulations references, 19
    notice requirement, 18
    waiver of notice requirement, 19
Appraisal Foundation, 177
Appraisal Standards Board, 177
Appraisal Subcommittee of the Federal Financial Institutions Examination Council, 177
Appraisals. See Real estate appraisals; Real estate ownership
Appraisers. See Real estate appraisals
Assessment, environmental, 96
Asset control programs. See Foreign asset controls
Asset growth, 7
Asset quality, 7
Assets, foreign. See Foreign asset controls
Audit system, internal, 6
Audits and attestation
    annual report, 22–23
    audit committee, 24–25
    audited financials, 23
    environmental, 96
    general requirements, 22
    holding company exception, 25–26
    independent public accountants (IPA), 24
    introduction and purpose, 22
    laws and regulations references, 26
    management report, 23–24
    See also Accounting standards
Automated clearinghouse (ACH) transactions, 76

B

Balance sheet assets, adjustment for, 56, 57–60
Bank Bribery Act, 28–29
Bank holding companies (BHC)
    market risk rule, 68
    minimum leverage ratio requirements, 69–70

Bank holding companies (BHC) *(continued)*
    and risk-weighted mutual funds, 60
    and Tier I capital, 52
    "well-capitalized," 73
Bank Holding Company Act (BHCA), 145
Bank premises, real estate ownership, 186–87
Bank Protection Act of 1968 (BPA)
    annual report to board, 33
    introduction and purpose, 32
    law and regulation references, 36
    recordkeeping requirements, 33, 35
    security issues, 32–33
    suspicious activity reporting, 33–36
Bank Secrecy Act, violations of, 34–35
Bank stock, loans secured by, 144–45, 154
Bankers, prohibited conduct of, 28
Bankers' acceptances, 139
Banking services for employees, Edge corporation, 114
Banks
    capital categories and, 72–73
    dividends and, 82–83
    market risk rule, 68
    minimum leverage ratio requirements, 69–70
    and risk-weighted mutual funds, 60
    and Tier I and II capital, 52
Basis points, more than 75, 38, 39
Basle Committee of Bank Supervisors (Basle Committee), 49, 50, 67
Below threshold, 175
Blocked assets, 101
Board of directors
    and business recovery planning, 44
    notification of SAR, 35
BOPEC composite rating, 51
Borrowing, Edge corporation, 114
Bribery. *See* Bank Bribery Act
Broker, deposit
    definition of, 39
    notification to FDIC, 41
Brokered deposits
    definition of, 38
    exceptions and waivers, 40
    introduction and purpose, 38
    laws and regulations references, 41
    prohibitions, 38
Brokers/dealers, special purpose loans to, 166
Business loans, real estate appraisals and, 175
Business recovery planning
    board of directors and management responsibilities, 44
    FFIEC Policy Statement, 44, 45
    introduction and purpose, 44
    planning process, 45–46
    references, 46
    service bureaus, 45

C

Call Reports, 12, 133, 153
    Schedule RC-M, 190

CAMEL ratings, 22, 26
Cap multiples, 78
Capital
    definition of, 51–53, 133
    PCA categories of, 38–39, 49, 70–72, 77
    tangible, 70
    total, 52
    total leverage, 70, 71*t*
    total risk-based, 70, 71*t*
    See also Tier I capital; Tier II capital; Tier III capital
Capital adequacy
    introduction and purpose, 49
    law and regulation references, 74
    minimum leverage ratio requirement, 69–70
    prompt corrective action (PCA). *See* Prompt corrective action (PCA)
    risk-based standards
        deductions, 53–54
        deferred tax assets, 55–56
        definition of capital, 51–53
        FAS 122 and interim rule on OMSRs, 55
        goodwill, 54
        introduction, 50
        qualifying intangible assets, 54–55
        risk management changes in 1998, 50–51
        servicing rights, 55
    risk-weighted assets
        assets sold with recourse, 60–61
        balance sheet assets, 56, 57–60
        calculation of credit equivalent amounts, 64–66
        credit conversion, 61–62
        exclusions, 63
        interest-rate, foreign-exchange, and commodity contracts, 63, 66
        interest rate risk (IRR), 66
        introduction, 56
        market risk rule, 67–69
        mutual funds, 60
        netting, 64
"Capital Adequacy Guidelines," 51, 116
Capital limitations test (12 U.S.C. 56), 82–83
Capital ratios, 38–39, 70–71
Capital stock and surplus, definition of, 12
Capitalization, Edge corporation, 116
Carrybacks, 56
Carryforwards, 56
Cattle, dairy, loans secured by, 140
Collateral
    affiliate transactions and, 12–13
    margin loans and, 165–66
    procedures, 134
    readily marketable, 133–34
Collections and payments, Edge corporation, 114
Commercial paper, discounting of, 139
Commitment fees, international loans, 123
Commitments to advance funds, 136–39
Commodity-related contracts, 63, 66
Common enterprise, 134
Community, management interlocks and, 158–59

Comparable terms, 15, 150
Compensation, fees, and benefits, 7
Competitive Equity Banking Act (CEBA) of 1987, 126, 127
Compliance. *See* Environmental assessments
Compliance exam, 3
Comprehensive Environmental Response, Compensation and Liability Act (CERCLA), 88, 89, 90, 92
Computer software & systems, recovery strategies for, 45–46
Confidentiality, of Suspicious Activity Report (SAR), 36
Conflict of interests. *See* Related interests
Consumer paper, discount of installment, 140
Contractual commitments, definition of, 133
Contribution, definition of, 170
Contributions, political, 170–71
Controlling interest, definition of, 149
Conversion factors, 61–62, 64–66
Core capital. *See* Tier I capital
Corporations, loans to, 134
Correspondent banks
    restrictions regarding, 153–54
    See also Savings associations
Correspondent capital, 105–07
"Correspondents," 104
Credit, extension of. *See* Extension of credit
Credit activities, Edge corporation, 114
Credit conversion factors. *See* Conversion factors
"Credit equivalent amount," 61, 64, 66
Credit exposure, 64–65
    calculation, 106–07
Credit underwriting, 6
Creditor exemption, secured. *See* Secured creditor exemption
Criminal Referral Forms, 33
Critically undercapitalized institutions, 49, 72
Current exposure method, 64–65
Customers, prohibited conduct of, 28
Customs, 102

D

Dairy cattle, loans secured by, 140
Daylight overdrafts. *See* Overdrafts, daylight
De minimis cap, 76, 78–79
Debt, subordinated, 53
Debt-for-equity swaps, 121
Debt previously contracted (DPC), 120, 145
Deferred tax assets, 55–56
Demand deposits, 192
Deposit accounts, segregated, loans secured by, 139
Deposit activities, Edge corporation, 113–14
Deposit broker
    definition of, 39
    notification to FDIC, 41
Depository Institution Management Interlocks Act, 158
Depository institutions, definition of, 192
Deposits. *See* Brokered deposits; Reserves on deposits
Director
    definition of, 148
    See also Board of directors
Disaster planning. *See* Business recovery planning

Disclosure, public, 153
Dividends
    introduction and purpose, 82
    laws and regulations references, 86
    limitations for banks
        capital limitations, 82–83
        earnings limitations, 82, 83
        "surplus surplus" transfers, 83
    limitations for savings associations
        OTS future revision, 84
        OTS regulations and future revision, 84
        OTS supervision restrictions, 85–86
        OTS tier dividends, 84–85
        OTS tier levels, 84
Documents of title, loans secured by, 139
Domestic branches, Edge corporations, 113

E

Earnings, 7
Earnings limitations test (12 U.S.C. 60), 82, 83
Economic sanctions. *See* Foreign asset controls
Edge and Agreement corporations, 110, 111, 112–14
    foreign investment activities, 116–21
    prudential restrictions on, 115–16
    reserve on deposits (Regulation D), 192
Elections, 170
Electronic Data Processing (EDP) Examination Handbook, The, 46
"Eligible country," 121
Emergency planning. *See* Business recovery planning
Employees, banking services for, 114
Environmental assessments, 96
    fiduciary liabilities, limitations on, 92–93
    hazards, 88–89
    introduction and purpose, 88
    laws and regulations references, 97
    liabilities, 89
    risk program, 95–97
    secured creditor exemption, 89, 90–92
    for underground storage tanks (USTs), 90, 93–95
Environmental audit, 96
Environmental compliance activities, permissible, secured creditor exemption for UST, 94–95
Environmental Protection Agency (EPA), 88, 90
Environmental review, 96
Environmental risk analysis, 96
Environmental risk program, 95–97
Equity derivative-related contracts, 63–64
Eurocurrency liabilities, 192, 193, 195
Exchange rate-related contracts, 63, 66
Executive officers
    definition of, 149
    filing of FFIEC 004, 154
    loan restrictions for, 152, 154–55
Expenditure, definition of, 170
Exposure limits, interbank liabilities and, 105
Extension of credit
    definition of, 150

Extension of credit *(continued)*
    to insiders. *See* Insiders, loans to
    See also Lending limits

F

FAS 109, 55
FAS 114, 53
FAS 115, 54
FAS 122, 55
FAS 125, 51
Federal agency, loans guaranteed by, 139
Federal Deposit Insurance Act, 6
    Section 36, 22
Federal Deposit Insurance Corporation (FDIC)
    annual reports filed with, 22–23
    audits and accounting standards, 22
    balance sheet assets, 58
    brokered deposits, 38, 40
    capital adequacy, 49, 52
    deposit brokers, 41
    dividends and, 82
    foreign operations, 110
    Interlocks Act, 158
    management interlocks, 160
    real estate lending standards, 180
Federal Deposit Insurance Corporation Improvement Act of 1991 (FDICIA)
    brokered deposit restrictions, 38
    loans to insiders, 148
    Section 121, 26
Federal Election Campaign Act, 170
Federal Financial Institutions Examination Council (FFIEC)
    Appraisal Subcommittee, 177
    FAS 122, 55
    Policy Statement on business recovery planning, 44, 45
Federal Home Loan Banks, 194
Federal National Mortgage Corporation, 188
Federal office, definition of, 170
Federal Reserve
    balance sheet assets, 58
    capital adequacy, 49, 52–53
    daylight overdrafts. *See* Overdrafts, daylight
    dividends, 83
    intangible assets, 55
    interbank liabilities, 104–7
    Interlocks Act, 158, 159, 160
    international banking operations, 110–24
    loans to insiders, 148
    margin loans, 164–67
    overdrafts. *See* Overdrafts, daylight
    Policy Statement, 76
    real estate lending standards, 180
    reserves on deposits, 192–95 (passim)
    Tier I leverage ratio, 51
    tying provisions, 199
    "well-capitalized" category for BHCs, 73
Federal Reserve Act
    reserves on deposits, 195

Federal Reserve Act *(continued)*
    Section 23A, 10–11, 13–14, 15–16
    Section 25(a), 113
    Section 23B, 10, 14–16
    Section 22(g), 148
    Section 22(h), 148
Federal Reserve Bank, 145, 194
Federal Reserve Bank Stock, balance sheet assets, 58
Federal Reserve System, 76
Federally chartered institutions, 170
Fedwire, 79, 80
    payment system risk and, 76
Fee appraisers, 178
FFIEC 004, 154
FFIEC Electronic Data Processing (EDP) Examination Handbook, The, 46
Fiduciary, real estate appraisals and, 176
Fiduciary and investment advisory activities, Edge corporation, 114
Fiduciary liabilities, limitations on, 92–93
Fiduciary purchase, 15
Finance leases, 128–29, 187
Financial Crimes Enforcement Network (FinCen), 36
Financial institutions, loans to, 139
Financials statements, audited, 23
FIRREA
    brokered deposit restrictions, 38
    dividend restrictions, 82
    management interlocks, 158
    Section 914, 18
Foreclosure
    postforeclosure and secured creditor exemption, 91–92
    preforeclosure and secured creditor exemption, 90–91
    underground storage tanks (USTs) and, 95
Foreign asset controls
    blocked assets, registration of, 101
    countries subject, 100
    introduction and purpose, 100
    laws and regulations references, 102
    penalties, 102
    reporting of transfers, 102
    scope of, 100–101
    specially designated persons and entities, 101
Foreign baking operations. *See* International banking operations
Foreign banks, daylight overdrafts, 80
Foreign branches of U.S. banking institutions, 110–12
Foreign exchange, Edge corporation, 114
Foreign exchange contracts, 63, 66
Foreign governments, loans to, 135
Foreign investments, Edge and Agreement corporation, 116–21
Foreign joint venture, 117
Foreign portfolio investments, 116, 117
Foreign subsidiary, 117
Form FR2900, 194, 195
Form FR 2950/2951, 195
Form FR 2910a, 195
Form FR 2910q, 194
Form U-1, 164–65
Free trade zone, 124
FSLIC Resolution Fund, 58, 59

Full-payout leases, 127–28

G

Generally accepted accounting principles (GAAP)
    audited financials, 23
    general accounting standards, 26
    other real estate owned (OREO), 188, 190
Gold bullion, 58
Good faith, 164–65
Goodwill, 54
Government real estate transactions, 175–76
Gross current exposure (NGR), 65
G.S.E., 175–76
Guide to the Federal Reserve's Payments System Risk Policy, The, 77

H

Hazards, environmental. *See* Environmental assessments
Home Owner's Loan Act, 128, 160

I

Independent public accountants (IPA), 24
Insiders, Loans to
    annual reports, 154
    correspondent bank restrictions, 153–54
    definitions, 148–50
    disclosures by banks, 153
    executive officer restrictions and reports, 152, 154–55
    introduction and purpose, 148
    laws and regulations references, 155
    loans secured by stock reports, 154
    maintenance of records, 153
    prohibitions, 150–52
    reports by banks, 153
    savings associations restrictions, 154–55
Intangible assets, deduction of, 54–55
Interagency Guidelines Establishing Standards for Safety and Soundness, 6
    agencies' existing authority, 7
    asset quality and earnings standards, 6, 7
    compliance plan, 7–8
    enforcement, 8
    introduction and purpose, 6
    operational and managerial standards, 6–7
    regulations and references, 8
Interbank liabilities
    correspondent capital, 105–07
    correspondent evaluation, 104–05
    exposure limits and monitoring, 105
    intraday exposures, 105
    introduction and purpose, 104
    laws and regulations references, 107
    policies and procedures, 104
    third-party, selection of correspondents by, 105
Interest rate exposure, 7
Interest rate-related contracts, 63, 66

Interest rate risk (IRR), 66–67
Interest rates, significantly higher, 39–40
Interlocks. *See* Management interlocks
Internal audit system, 6
Internal controls and information systems, 6
International banking facility (IBF), 123–24
International banking operations
    accounting for fees on international loans, 122–23
    allocated transfer risk reserves (ATRR), 121–22
    changes in, 110–11, 117–21 (passim)
    Edge and Agreement corporations. *See* Edge and Agreement corporations
    foreign branches of U.S. banking institutions, 110–12
    international banking facilities (IBFs), 123–24
    introduction and purpose, 110
    laws and regulations references, 124
    reporting and disclosure third parties, 122
    supervision and reporting, 121
International loans, fees on, 122–23
Intraday exposures, 105
Intraday overdrafts, 140
Investment advisory activities, Edge corporation, 114

J

Joint agency rule, CDRI Act and 1996
"Joint rule," 158–59
    exemptions, 160–61
Joint venture, foreign, 117

L

Large customer, definition of, 25
Lease financing
    CEBA Leases, 127
    federal savings associations requirements, 128
    finance leases, 128–29
    full-payout, 127–28
    general leases, 129
    general rule, 126–27
    introduction and purpose, 126
    laws and regulations references, 129
    national bank requirements, 126
    salvage powers, 129
Leases
    finance, 187
    real estate appraisals and, 175
Lending limits
    collateral procedures, 134
    combining loans to separate borrowers, 134–35
    commitments to advance funds, 136–39
    definitions, 132–34
    Edge corporation, 115–16
    exceptions and exclusions, 139–40
    general limitations, 132
    to insiders, 151
    introduction and purpose, 132
    laws and regulations references, 141
    nonconforming loans, 135–36

Lending limits *(continued)*
    renewals, 138–39
        savings association exceptions, 140–41
Lending standards; *See* Real estate lending standards
Leverage ratio, minimum, 69–70
Leverage ratio, Tier I, 51
Liens, 175
Liquid funds, Edge corporation, 114
Livestock, loans secured by, 140
Loan commitment fees, international loans, 123
Loan documentation, 6
    environmental risk program, 96–97
Loan oversight activities, permissible, secured creditor exemption for UST, 94–95
Loan to value (LTV), 181–82
Loan work-out activities, 95
Loans
    insider. *See* Insiders, loans to
    legally unenforceable, 140
    margin. *See* Margin loans
    political, 170
    secured by bank stock, 145
    special purpose, 166
    See also Lending limits
Loans and extension of credit, definition of, 132
Low-quality assets, 12, 13

M

Management Consignment exemption, 161
Management interlocks
    applicability, 158
    change in circumstances, 161
    exemptions, 160–61
    "Interlocks Act," 158, 159, 160
    introduction and purpose, 158
    laws and regulations references, 161
    prohibitions, 158–59
    relationships permitted by statute, 159–60
"Management official," definition of, 158
Management report, 23–24
Managing banking institutions, international loans and, 123
Margin loans
    coverage-purpose loan, 164
    decline in value of collateral, 165
    exempted transactions, 166–67
    introduction and purpose, 164
    laws and regulations references, 167
    maximum loan value, 164
    proposals, 167
    purpose statement (Form U-1), 164–65
    single-credit rule, 165–66
    special purpose loans to brokers/dealers, 166
    withdrawals/substitutions of cash or collateral, 166
Margin requirements, affiliate transactions and, 12–13
Margin stock
    definition of, 164
    See also Margin loans
Market risk rule, 67–69

Market Valuation Model, 67
Maximum loan value, 164
Means test, 135
Money laundering, and filing SAR, 34–35
Money market deposit accounts (MMDAs), 192
Monitoring
    environmental risk program, 97
    interbank liabilities and, 105
Mortgage-servicing assets ("MSAs"), 55
Mortgage servicing rights (MSR), 54
Mutual fund holdings, risk weighting, 60

N

NASDAQ, National Market System, 164
National Bank Act
    Section 12 U.S.C. 24 (Seventh), 126, 127–28
    Section 12 U.S.C. 24 (Tenth), 126
National Credit Union Administration Central Liquidity Facility, 194
National securities exchange, 164
"Negative" pledge agreement, 164
Net debit caps, 76–77, 78
Net lease basis, 126
Netting, 64
Nonconforming loans, 135–36
Nonpersonal time deposits, 193
Note issuance facilities (NIFs), 62
NOW accounts, 192

O

OAEM rated assets, 13
OECD countries
    banks in, balance sheet assets, 58, 59
    definition of, 58*n.1*
Office of Comptroller of the Currency (OCC)
    capital adequacy, 52
    Interlocks Act, 158
    lease financing, 126, 127
    nonconforming loans, 135–36
    real estate lending standards, 180
    real estate ownership, 186–90 (*passim*)
Office of Foreign Assets Control (OFAC), 100–102
Office of Thrift Supervision (OTS)
    capital adequacy, 52
    dividend regulations, 84–86
    independent audits, 22
    Interlocks Act, 158
    lease financing, 126, 128
    loans to insiders, 154
    Market Valuation Model, 67
    proposed interest rate risk (IRR), 66–67
    real estate lending standards, 180
    Thrift Bulletin, 67
Originated mortgage servicing rights (OMSR), 55
OTC. *See* Over-the-counter (OTC)
Other real estate owned (OREO). *See* Real estate ownership, other real estate owned (OREO)

Over-the-counter (OTC)
　derivatives, 68, 69
　stocks, 164
Overdrafts
　daylight
　　administration of, 79
　　cap multiples, 78
　　covered institutions, 76
　　de minimis cap, 76, 78–79
　　foreign banks, 80
　　introduction and purpose, 76
　　net debit caps, 76–77, 78
　　pricing, 79–80
　　references, 80
　　self-assessment cap, 77–78
　　zero cap, 79
　loans to insiders, 150–51
Overdrafts, intraday, 140

P

Partnerships, loans to, 135
Payment system risks, 76
Payments and collections, Edge corporation, 114
Perpetual preferred stock, 52
Person, definition of, 132
Points, basis, more than 75, 38, 39
Policies, environmental risk program, 96
Political action committee (PAC), 170–71
Political contributions, 170–71
Political loans, 170
Political subdivision general obligations, 140
Portfolio investments, foreign, 116, 117
Postforeclosure activities, secured creditor exemption and, 91–92
Pre-approval, of credit to insiders, 150
Pre-lending activities, permissible, secured creditor exemption for UST, 94
Preferred stock, perpetual, 52
Preforeclosure activities, secured creditor exemption and, 90–91
PricewaterhouseCoopers Regulatory Advisory Service, 3
Principal shareholders
　definition of, 149
　filing of FFIEC 004, 154
Prohibition, 144
Prompt Corrective Action (PCA)
　capital categories, 38–39, 49, 70–72, 77
　determining a bank or thrift capital category, 72–73
　introduction, 70
Prudential restrictions, on Edge corporations, 115–16
"Prudential standards," 104–5
Public disclosure, 153
Purchased credit card relationship (PCCR), 54, 55
Purpose loans/credit, 164, 165–66
Purpose test, 135

Q

Quarterly Report of Selected Deposits, Vault Cash and Reservable Liabilities, (Form FR 2910q), 194

R

Readily marketable collateral, 133–34
Real estate appraisals
　appraiser independence, 177–78
　certification/licensing requirements, 177
　introduction and purpose, 174
　laws and regulations references, 178
　nonappraisal evaluations, 176
　OREO, 190
　standards for, 177
　transactions covered, 174
　transactions requiring, 174–76
　transactions requiring certified appraiser, 176–77
　transactions requiring certified or licensed appraiser, 177
Real estate lending standards
　exceptions and exclusions, 182–83
　guidelines applicability, 180
　introduction and purpose, 180
　laws and regulations references, 183
　policy formation, 180–81
　supervisory LTV limits, 181–82
　supervisory review, 183
Real estate notes, 175
Real estate ownership
　bank premises, 186–87
　finance leases, 187
　future expansion, 187
　general limitation, 186
　introduction and purpose, 186
　law and regulation references, 190
　other real estate owned (OREO), 187, 188
　　accounting requirements, 190
　　appraisals, 189–90
　　disposal of, 188–89
　　holding period, 189
　　improvements to, 189–90
Real estate related financial transaction, 174
"Recourse" rule revision, 50–51
Refinancing, real estate appraisals and, 175
Regulation D, 192–93 (*passim*)
Regulation F, 104–7
Regulation K, 110–24, 119, 122
Regulation O, 112, 148, 149, 154
Regulation U, 164–65
　exemptions, 165–66
　proposed changes, 166
Regulation Y, 117, 118, 119
Regulatory Advisory Service, PricewaterhouseCoopers, 3
Regulatory Reporting Handbook, The, 35
Regulatory Standards exemption, 160
Related interests, 153, 154–55
　definition of, 149
Relevant Metropolitan Statistical Area (RMSA), 159
Renewals, real estate appraisals and, 175
Report FFIEC 004, 154
Report of Certain Eurocurrency Transactions (FR 2950/2951), 195
Report of Condition and Income, 12, 151

Report of Selected Deposits, Vault Cash and Reservable Liabilities, Quarterly (Form FR 2910q), 194
Report of Total Deposits and Reservable Liabilities, Annual, (Form FR 2910a), 195
Report of Transaction Accounts, Other Deposits and Vault Cash (Form FR2900), 194
Reserves on deposits
    1998 changes to, 195
    affected institutions, 192
    computation of, 195
    definitions, 192–93
    introduction and purpose, 192
    laws and regulations references, 196
    maintenance of reserves, 193–94
    reporting requirements, 194–95
    reserve requirements, 192, 193
Resolution Trust Corporation (RTC), balance sheet assets, 58, 59
Resource Conservation and Recovery Act of 1986, 88
Restructured international loans, 122
Review, environmental, 96
Revolving underwriting facilities (RUFs), 62
Right to Privacy Act, safe harbor of, 35
Risk-based capital. *See* Capital adequacy, risk-based standards
Risk management reports, 7
Risk-weighted assets. *See* Capital adequacy, risk-weighted assets

S

Safe Harbor, 35
Safekeeping agreement, 164
Sallie Mae, 140
Salvage powers, leasing, 129
Sanctions. *See* Foreign asset controls
Savings accounts, 192
Savings associations
    affiliate transactions restrictions for, 15–16
    balance sheet assets, 58
    dividends and, 84–86
    FIRREA restrictions, 82
    insider loans and, 153–55
    leasing requirements for Federal, 128
    lending limit exceptions, 140–41
    minimum leverage ratio requirements, 69–70
    OTS requirements for, 67, 82, 84–86
    and risk-weighted mutual funds, 60
    and Tier I capital, 52
Schedule RC-M, 190
Section 36, 22
Section 56, 60, 82
Section 121, 26
Section 12 U.S.C. 84, 132, 136, 139
Section 12 U.S.C. 24 (Seventh), 126, 127–28
Section 12 U.S.C. 24 (Tenth), 126
Section 25(a), 113
Section 22(g), 148
Section 22(h), 148
Secured creditor exemption, 89, 90–92
    for underground storage tanks (USTs), 90, 93–95
Secured loans, 132, 139

Securities exchange, 164
Security
    devices, 32–33
    See also Foreign asset controls
Security officer, 32, 33
Security program, 32, 33
Segregated deposit accounts, loans secured by, 139
Self-assessment cap, 77–78
"Senior executive officer," definition of, 18
Service bureaus, business recovery planning and, 45
Share draft accounts, 192
Significantly higher interest rates, definition of, 39–40
Significantly undercapitalized institutions, 49, 72
Single-credit rule, 165–66
Special purpose loans, 166
"Specially Designated Nationals and Blocked Entities," 101
Specially Designated Nationals and Blocked Persons, 101
"Specially Designated Nationals" (SDNs), 101
"Specially Designated Terrorists" (SDTs), 101
Staff appraisers, 177
State chartered institutions, 170
State subdivision general obligations, 140
Statutory veto power, over directors and executives, 18
Stock
    bank, 144–45, 154
    margin, 164. *See also* Margin loans
Storage tanks, underground (USTs), 88, 90, 93–95
Student Loan Marketing Association (Sallie Mae), 140
Subordinated debt, 53
Subsidiary, foreign, 117
"Superfund" statute, 88
Supervisory composite rating, 77t
Supplementary capital. *See* Tier II capital
Surplus, definition of, 133
"Surplus surplus" transfers, 83
Suspicious Activity Report (SAR), 33–34
    confidentiality of, 36
    filing of forms, 34–36
    mailing instructions, 36

T

"Tangible capital requirement," 70
"Terrorists, Specially Designated" (SDTs), 101
Third parties, reporting and disclosure of, 122
Third-party credit enhancements, 50–51
Third-party evaluations and correspondents, 105
Thrift Bulletin (OTS), 67
Thrifts, capital categories and, 72–73
Tier dividends, OTS, 84–86
Tier I capital, 12, 50, 54, 133
    definition of, 51–52
Tier I leverage ratio, 51
Tier I risk-based capital, 70, 71t
Tier II capital, 12, 50, 133
    definition of, 52–53
Tier III capital, 68–69
Time deposits, 192
    nonpersonal, 193

Total capital, 52
Total leverage capital, 70, 71t
Total risk-based capital, 70, 71t
Training, environmental risk program, 95–96
Transaction accounts, definition of, 192
Transfer risk, 121
"Troubled" condition of financial institutions, 18
Tying provisions
    exceptions, 199
    introduction and purpose, 198
    laws and regulations references, 200
    private lawsuits, 199
    prohibited arrangements, 198–99

U

Unauthorized loans, insiders and, 152
Undercapitalized institutions, 38–39, 49, 71–72
Underground storage tanks (USTs), 88, 90, 93–95
Underwriter, purchase from affiliate as, 15
Underwriting, credit, 6
"Undivided profits," 82–83
Unenforceable loans, 140
Uniform Financial Institutions Rating System, 18
"Unimpaired capital and surplus," 151
Unsecured loans, 132, 175
U.S. Customs Office, 102
U.S. Department of the Treasury
    Financial Crimes Enforcement Network (FinCEN), 36

U.S. Department of the Treasury *(continued)*
    Office of Foreign Assets Control (OFAC), 100–102
U.S. foreign policy, 100
U.S. obligations, loans secured by, 139
U.S. Secret Service, Financial Crimes Division, 36

V

Value-at-risk (VAR), 68, 69
Vault cash, 195
Veto power, over directors and executives, 18

W

Waivers
    brokered deposits, 40
    capital exposure limit, 107
Well-capitalized institutions, 38–39, 49, 71, 73
Wire transfer systems, 76
Work-out activities, secured creditor exemption for UST, 95

Y

Y-9C Report, 68

Z

Zero cap, 79